Managing Money

A Video Arts Guide

Video Arts is the world's leading producer and distributor of training videos. There are now over 150 Video Arts titles in daily use by some 100,000 organisations worldwide, spread throughout 60 countries. Between them they have won over 200 awards in major international festivals.

Video Arts programmes combine the highest standards of production excellence with the maximum training impact. The quality of the research, writing, creativity and production is exceptional, and the Mandarin Video Arts series is designed to make available this expertise, entertainment and long-established success in handy book form.

*Other Video Arts books
available in Mandarin*

Are You Organised?
Working With People
Are You a Leader?
Doing Business on the Phone
Success at Selling

Managing Money

Finance for Non-Financial Managers

Video Arts

*Cartoons by Don Seed, Tony Hart,
Shaun Williams and Chris Allies*

Mandarin

This book is based on the following Video Arts training videos and accompanying Briefcase Booklets:

The Balance Sheet Barrier by Antony Jay
The Control of Working Capital by Antony Jay
Cost, Profit & Break-even by Antony Jay
Budgeting; film script by Graeme Garden; booklet by John Hemingway

A Mandarin Paperback
MANAGING MONEY

First published in Great Britain 1994
by Mandarin Paperbacks
an imprint of Reed Books Ltd
Michelin House, 81 Fulham Road, London SW3 6RB
and Auckland, Melbourne, Singapore and Toronto

Reprinted 1995

Copyright © Video Arts Ltd 1994
Illustrations © Video Arts Ltd

A CIP catalogue record for this title
is available from the British Library
ISBN 0 7493 1951 8

Printed and bound in Great Britain
by Cox & Wyman Ltd, Reading, Berkshire

This book is sold subject to the condition
that it shall not, by way of trade or otherwise,
be lent, resold, hired out, or otherwise circulated
without the publisher's prior consent in any form
of binding or cover other than that in which
it is published and without a similar condition
including this condition being imposed
on the subsequent purchaser.

Contents

1
7 The balance sheet barrier

2
73 The control of working capital

3
95 Cost, profit and break-even

4
115 Budgeting

1 The balance sheet barrier

You are a literate and intelligent person. You're no Einstein, but you can manage costings and budgets quite satisfactorily.

There is, however, one area that you do not seem able to get to grips with: the whole grey and foggy world of accountancy conventions and financial mumbo-jumbo, the world of balance sheets, capital and revenue transactions, working capital and the like. You feel slightly guilty about this, because you know it lies at the heart of every business. You also feel slightly resentful because, deep down, you have a suspicion that it isn't really all that complicated. It's just that no one has ever explained it to you in simple language, without all the accountants' jargon. You are quite right. It is indeed basically very simple. But some very sophisticated people come unstuck because they do not really understand how it all works.

So let's meet one of them. His name is Carruthers. He is very sophisticated, very grand, but extremely hazy about accountants' jargon. So to get a little help he consults the low-born, crude, but highly successful Rita Scroggs.

> **Carruthers:** My name is Julian Carruthers. I am deputy long range planning executive of Universal International. We have companies all over the world. We turn over £700,000 million a year. Or is it £700 million? Or dollars? Anyway, something like that.
> **Scroggs:** I am Rita Scroggs of Scroggs

Manufacturing. I have a wooden shed in Brixton. Last year I turned over £301,427.53p.

Carruthers: I work on the fifty-first floor of Universal House, and I am widely respected throughout the Corporation.

Scroggs: I work in a corner of the shed, and my team think I'm a bitch.

Carruthers: I am a highly sophisticated manager. I know all about TQM, Theory X and Theory Y, Hygiene Factors, Management Matrices and of course the Hierarchy of Needs. The only thing I do not understand is finance.

Scroggs: I am a highly unsophisticated manager. I don't know what the hell he is talking about. But I watch the figures like a hawk.

Carruthers: My colleagues are highly sophisticated managers too. They do not understand finance either. All of us feel slightly uneasy about admitting it, so we have a gentleman's agreement not to refer to it. We leave the financial arrangements to the accounting people just as we leave the catering arrangements to the canteen people. We believe in trusting people.

Scroggs: I do not trust anybody, but then, fortunately I am not a gentleman. I cut my own sandwiches and I do my own accounts.

Carruthers: I would lose face if I admitted to anyone in the Corporation that I do not understand finance, since I am constantly approving financial statements, draft accounts and balance sheets.

Scroggs: If I didn't understand finance I would not lose face. But I would lose all my money.

Carruthers: I have come to this person for help because she is so basic and unspoiled that she will use

short, simple words that I can understand; and not the obscure mumbo-jumbo that accountants try to frighten you with.
Scroggs: Because I am basic and unspoiled I am very flattered by his attention. But just what is it he doesn't understand?
Carruthers: Well, I understand a great deal about management. But pitifully little about how business actually works.
Scroggs: Right! Later on I'll tell him about working capital, P & L accounts and cash flow forecasts. But we'll start by looking at a balance sheet. It is the window which reveals the business.
Carruthers: It is not the window which reveals the business. It is the blind drawn by accountants to keep us managers in the dark.
Scroggs: Then for the time being we will forget about the balance sheet. We'll just talk about money. In business, money only does two things. It comes in, and it goes out. There are two basic things you have to know:

> Where did it come in from?
> And where did it go out to?
> All right?

Carruthers: Yes, yes. I understand that.
Scroggs: Good, so let's begin with where it comes from.

Say you're starting a business. There's only two places you can get money from.

The first is by risking your own, and perhaps getting some other people to share the risk with you. That money is called 'share capital' or the 'equity', and the shareholders are the owners of the business and share all its profits.

The second way to get money is to borrow it, on a long term basis, and pay interest. That's called 'loan capital'.

Carruthers: Light is beginning to dawn. There are only two places money can come from: share capital and loan capital. The owners' money and the money that they borrow from someone else.

Scroggs: You've got it. Now you've raised the money. Where are you going to put it?

Carruthers: I am going to put it . . . into . . . the business.

Scroggs: I see; and what part of the business?

Carruthers: Ah, into the part of the business, er, that . . . you tell me to.

Scroggs: Right. Well, just as there are only two places money can come from, there are only two places money can go out to. First, you can put it into things you mean to keep: buildings, machinery, cars, furniture. All those are called Fixed Assets.

And second, you can put it into things you mean to sell: raw materials, piece-parts, packaging materials and so on. That money is called Working Capital.

Carruthers: Ah, I've heard of that.

Scroggs: So there is the basis of every business: the two places money can come from – share capital, risking your own, and loan capital, borrowing someone else's – and the two places it can go to: fixed assets, things you mean to keep, and working capital, things you mean to sell.

Carruthers: I now know, which I knew all along, but did not know that I knew, that a business is based on cash and that you start by saying where you got it and what you did with it. I now understand how a business works.

Scroggs: He does not understand how a business works because he does not understand working capital.

Carruthers: I cannot imagine why she thinks I do not understand working capital.

Scroggs: Then let us ask him three questions. Does the rent of the factory come out of working capital? Does bank interest come out of working capital? Do wages come out of working capital?

Carruthers: . . . Well, I can now understand why she thinks I do not understand working capital.

Scroggs: Do you want a lot of money in working capital, or a little?

Carruthers: All capital is good, so I want a lot.

Scroggs: In fact, you want as little money as possible tied up in working capital.

Carruthers: I have changed my mind. As little as possible. Quite, yes, yes, I see. No, I don't. I do not understand working capital. Not at all.

Scroggs: Right. Well, all businesses are the same. You put money in, and you get money out. Sometimes you get less money out than you put in. Then you go bust. Sometimes you get more money out. Then you're in business. Is that clear?

Carruthers: Yes, yes. I'm not stupid, you know.

Scroggs: Oh good. Now we know about the fixed assets, the things you mean to keep. They're obvious. But they can't make money on their own. To make money you need working capital.

You need it to buy raw materials, and you need it

to pay the workforce to turn the raw materials into something you can sell at a profit. You need it to pay the overheads – administrative staff, electricity, rates, insurance, postage, telephone and all that. Not to mention the interest on the money you borrowed. Then you can start to make money.
Carruthers: How?
Scroggs: Well, look at Scroggs Manufacturing. I make teaspoons. All I do is spend £60 on ten kilos of light alloy strip on Monday, change its shape, and sell it for £300 on Friday. I buy another ten kilos of light alloy strip. I pay the workforce. I pay the overheads and I put a bit aside. And I keep a bit for myself. The bit I put aside goes into Reserves and Investments. The bit I keep I pay myself as a Dividend. But I'll leave explanations for a little later.

Summary: Money, where it comes from and where it goes

Start by doing two things. The first is to imagine yourself the proprietor of a business. It can be a very small business, occupying no more than a shed at the bottom of the garden. What matters is that it is yours, and that you look at it with a proprietor's eye and ask the questions that are always in the proprietor's mind:

- How much is it worth at the moment?
- How secure is it?
- How much a year is it bringing in?

Once you start to look at business in this way and ask these sort of questions, you are on the way to understanding all the jargon and mumbo-jumbo.

The second thing you have to do is forget about paper. Forget about figures, accounts and statements. Just think about money. Your money.

There are two basic things you have to know about your money:

- Where did it come from?
- Where did it go?

WHERE DID IT COME FROM?

When you start a business there are only two places you can get money from:

1. Use your own.
2. Borrow someone else's.

Use your own

If there are several of you, you go shares. Your own money is called 'shares' or 'equity' and the amount you start with is called **Share Capital**.

Borrow Someone Else's

This is called 'loan' or 'debt' or 'debenture capital' and is normally listed as **Loan Capital**.

After you've been going for a year or so, you may have some profits. Some you share out. Some you keep in the business: you plough back.

Plough Back Profit

This is called 'retained earnings', 'undistributed profit', 'reinvestment', 'internally generated finance', etc, but it is entered on the balance sheet as **Reserves**.

Now you already understand half the balance sheet. It's the half that tells you where the money came from, and it can only have come from three places.

    a Share Capital (your own money).
    b Loan Capital (someone else's money).
    c Reserves (ploughed back profit).

WHERE DID IT GO TO?

When you start a business, there are only two kinds of things you can spend your money on:

    1 Things you mean to keep.
    2 Things you mean to sell.

Things You Mean To Keep
You mean to keep the buildings, desks, computers, machine tools, delivery vans, ash trays and the Managing Director's car. These are called **Fixed Assets**.

Things You Mean To Sell
All the raw materials that you intend to manufacture, assemble, pack with, decorate with, and which become more and more valuable as you spend more and more on turning them into finished goods. Money tied up in raw materials, work in progress and finished goods not yet sold is called **Working Capital**. (Of course you use a lot of this money to pay people for their work on the raw materials. But as far as you are concerned, £5 paid to a machine operator is £5 added to the cost, and so the value, of the material they have machined. You've still got the money, but it's no longer in bank-notes – it's in the added value of the product you're going to sell.)

SAVINGS

Profit not distributed or ploughed back can be put into a building society, national savings, deposit account, shares, commodities, gilts, or what you will. It will be listed in the balance sheet as **Investments**.

Now you understand the other half of the balance sheet. It's the half that tells you where the money has gone to, and it can only have gone to three places.

a Fixed Assets.
b Working Capital.
c Investments.

So now we can draw up the basic balance sheet:

	£	Financed by:	£
Fixed Assets	1,000	Share Capital	1,000
Working Capital	1,000	Loan Capital	1,000
Investments	1,000	Reserves	1,000
	3,000		3,000

Or as some accountants prefer to express it:

	£		£
Fixed Assets	1,000	Share Capital	1,000
Investments	1,000	Reserves	1,000
Working Capital	1,000		
	3,000		
Loan Capital	(1,000)		
Net Assets	2,000	Shareholders' Funds	2,000

These two versions are just alternative ways of looking at the same thing. We'll look at the difference later on.

Note: The Differences between Loan Capital and Share Capital

Loan capital and share capital are the only two kinds of money you can start a business with. What exactly is the difference? The principal and obvious difference is that share capital belongs to you and loan capital belongs to someone else, but in detail it works like this:

Loan Capital is, in practice, usually a long term loan which the lender – let's say the bank – cannot claim back until the end of the period they lent it to you for. (Obviously you don't want to buy a battery of machine tools with it and then have them demand the money back next Friday.) Long fixed-term loan capital of this sort is often obtained from a number of people under a borrowing agreement called a 'debenture deed' and the lenders are called 'debenture holders'. The chief characteristics of loan capital are:

1. The interest is a legal charge on the company which has to be paid when it is due, just like the rent. What is more you have to pay the interest on the total sum lent for the whole period of the loan. Even if your account at the bank is in credit to the full amount, you are not entitled to pay it off until the term is completed. This is why it is different from an overdraft – with an overdraft you only pay interest to the extent that you are in the red at any given period.
2. There is a date on which the lender is entitled to have their money back and you are legally bound

to return it to them, unless of course they agree to extend the term of the loan.

3 The loan is repayable at its original money value. If you borrowed £10,000, you repay £10,000, irrespective of the rise and fall in the value of the company (or of money, for that matter).

4 The return of the loan at the end of its term is a legal charge on the company, and if the company will not or cannot repay it, the lender (along with any other creditors) is entitled to put a receiver into the company and if necessary force the sale of assets or securities. If the company is wound up or broken up, the proceeds go to repay secured loans before giving back to the shareholders any of their original capital.

Share Capital is what remains after all loans and debts have been paid. It is also called the 'equity', and it is the property of the shareholders in a proportion expressed by the number of shares each holds.

The chief characteristics of share capital are:

1 No interest has to be paid on shares, and the shareholders have no legal entitlement to any return on their investment. Instead, they own what is left (if anything) each year after the payment of all debts, costs and taxes, and can decide whether to put it back into the business ('reserves') or divide it up amongst the shareholders in proportion to their shareholdings ('dividends').

2 Shareholders have no right to take their money out of the business. All they can do is sell their shares, and if they cannot find anyone to buy them, that's just too bad.

3 The shares do not have a fixed value. They are worth what people will pay for them. If the company dwindles in value, they may sink to nothing – and on the other hand, if it really takes off they may be worth many times the money the shareholders originally subscribed.
4 The share capital does not ever have to be returned and if the company is wound up or broken up the shareholders get nothing until every other debt has been paid in full.

Those then are the main differences. Obviously the ratio of loan to share capital in a company has important implications, since you do not have to pay dividends on share capital if you do not make a profit, but you have to pay interest on loan capital even if you make a loss. But we shall be looking at this later, when we come to examine what is called the 'gearing' of a business.

Scroggs: Well, are you happy so far?
Carruthers: No, I'm not happy.
Scroggs: Why not?
Carruthers: It's so simple I am getting suspicious. And, to be frank, I'm not certain I have mastered working capital.
Scroggs: Well, let's look a bit closer. Take that light alloy strip I buy on Monday for £60.

On Tuesday I pay Harry £20 for stamping it into blanks. Now I've got £80 invested in stamped blanks.

On Wednesday I pay Sharon £20 to press the blanks into spoons. Now I've got £100 invested in pressed spoons.

On Thursday I pay Bill £20 to pack the spoons and send them to the collection bay. Now I've got £120 invested in packed spoons.

On Friday I pay all the bills for the week's overheads. They come to £100. So now I've got £220 invested in a crate of teaspoons. That's £220 tied up in working capital.

And on Friday afternoon the customer collects the spoons and pays £300 for them. So I have recovered my investment of £220 in working capital and made £80 profit.

Carruthers: I see. It's really a sort of cash merry-go-round. You put in cash and get raw material. You put in more cash to get it stamped, pressed and packed. You put in more cash to pay the overheads. Then you sell it and get your working capital back; and a bit over. Then you start again.

See? A cash merry-go-round.

Scroggs: For a sophisticated manager, that's quite a sensible statement.

Carruthers: Ah! I've got something right. I now understand working capital. Sort of. I see that working capital is all the money tied up in things that you hope one day to sell to customers. What I cannot see is how she can live on £80 a week.

Scroggs: I cannot live on £80 a week.

Carruthers: I have got something else right.

Scroggs: I do not have to live on £80 a week.

Carruthers: Ah. She has a private income.
Scroggs: I do not have a private income. What has not struck him is that I have a five-day week. I do not buy light alloy strip on Mondays only. I buy it every day. So every day Harry stamps out ten kilos of blanks. Every day Sharon presses ten kilos of spoons. Every day Bill packs the spoons and takes them to the collection bay. Every day a customer collects the spoons and pays for them. It is a continuous process all through the year. So the cash merry-go-round goes on all the time.

Now, because he is sophisticated he will now be able to tell me how much I clear a week.
Carruthers: This is the sort of problem I am good at, because I am sophisticated. Ah, she clears £80 a day five days a week. So she clears £400 a week.
Scroggs: He may be sophisticated but he is as thick as two short planks. He has walked right into my trap. You say I clear £400 a week?
Carruthers: £400 is correct.
Scroggs: OK. If I spent £60 a day on strip metal, how much do I spend a week?
Carruthers: £300.
Scroggs: If I pay Harry £20 a day for blanking, what do I pay him a week?
Carruthers: £100.
Scroggs: And Sharon for pressing?
Carruthers: £100.
Scroggs: And Bill for packing?
Carruthers: £100.
Scroggs: And overheads?
Carruthers: £100.
Scroggs: So how much goes out every week?

Carruthers: £700.

Scroggs: And if I collect £300 on Monday, Tuesday, Wednesday, Thursday and Friday, how much do I collect a week?

Carruthers: Five times £300 is £1500.

Scroggs: So if I collect £1500 a week and spend £700 a week, how much do I clear?

Carruthers: £800. I have fallen into a trap. I said she cleared £400 a week but she has proved she clears £800 a week. I do not see how she has done this. But I do see how she can live on £800 a week.

Scroggs: I have trapped him because he does not understand about overheads.

I have to pay £100 a week overheads whether I make one consignment of teaspoons or five consignments. He charged a week's overheads on to every day's consignment, so he put four times £100 too much on my costs. But you only pay a week's overheads once a week.

Carruthers: I have learnt my lesson. I see that overheads don't multiply like materials and labour. She only pays her overheads once a week. So the more consignments she produces each week, the more profit she makes on each consignment, because they divide up the overhead into smaller portions. I now understand working capital.

Summary: Working Capital and the Merry-go-round

We have looked at the six possible headings in a balance sheet: three where money comes from, and three where it can go to.

Five of them are pretty obvious as soon as you see what they mean.

One of them isn't. The one that isn't obvious is **Working Capital**, and what this chapter is largely about is Working Capital.

You have just started a business. You are going to manufacture cheap metal teaspoons for the catering trade. You rent a building at the bottom of the garden which will serve as a factory workshop. Your own sitting room will serve as the office. You put your savings into buying a Super Spoonmaster Fine Blanking Machine, a Master Cutler Spoon Press and a set of teaspoon-pressing dies to go with it. Those are all the fixed assets you need. You are fully equipped. So off you go.

But you don't.

You don't go because you haven't got anyone to operate the Blanking Machine or the Press, you haven't got any metal to make the spoons with, you haven't insured the building or the machine, you have no lubricant and you have no telephone to call the hotels and restaurants to find out if they need teaspoons of your sort at your price. You will also need electricity to run the machine and heat the workshop, and money for rent, rates, water, paper, postage and advertising.

Of course all this will be paid for by the money your customers pay you for your teaspoons, once you get going. But you work out that you will need to spend £1000 on labour, materials and overheads before the money starts to come back.

So you borrow it from the bank (if you don't raise it from shareholders) and start up. You have then invested a further £1000 in **Working Capital**.

Now, let's suppose all goes well; you sell lots of teaspoons and pay back the £1000 to the bank. Does that mean you now have no working capital?

No. It only means you have replaced loan capital with share capital. You still have cash tied up in materials, work in progress and unsold goods. However, it's hard to see because it's moving. It's on the money-go-round.

The money-go-round is the key to understanding working capital, which is the heart of a business, the engine that drives the whole enterprise.

The money-go-round starts with cash, and ends with it.

If it ends with less cash than you started with, you lose money and eventually go bankrupt.

So the purpose of the money-go-round is to turn a sum of cash into a larger sum of cash.

In your case, you buy 10 kilos of one-inch light alloy strip metal for £60 and sell it for £300. (When you sell it, it's in short lengths of a special shape and you call it teaspoons.)

All the expenses you incur – wages, fuel, rent, transport, advertising, telephone – are simply to make your £60 cash increase its value as it goes round the money-go-round.

On the first day you turn £60 cash into strip metal. Heat, light, fuel, rent, insurance, postage and phone calls for the day – while the metal is sitting in 'Goods Inwards' – come to another £20. You've spent £80 on the raw material altogether.

On the next day Harry stamps it all into blanks. Harry's wages for the day cost £20. Another day's bills, another £20. So the stamped blanks have cost £120.

At the end of the third day, Sharon has pressed the blanks into spoons. Sharon's wages for the day cost £20, and the overheads were £20 again. So the finished spoons have cost £160.

At the end of the fourth day, Bill has packed the spoons and delivered them to the collection bay. Bill's wages for the day were £20 and the overheads were £20 and so the finished spoons delivered to the collection bay have cost £200.

On the fifth day, while you are waiting for the customer to arrive, you still have to pay £20 in overheads – making a total of £220 invested in the crate of spoons before anything comes back.

At the end of the fifth day, a van driver comes from Imperial Hotels Ltd, collects the spoons and pays for them with six £50 notes.

So you made £80 profit on the £220 you paid out. Not bad for five days. And on Monday, you can turn the cash back into strip metal again and carry on round the money-go-round.

But of course a factory keeps going all the time. You didn't set all this up just to make one consignment of spoons. Each day you bought another £60 worth of strip metal, each day Harry stamped out 10 kilos of blanks, each day Sharon pressed the previous day's blanks into spoons, each day Bill packed and delivered a consignment of spoons to the collection bay, and each day a customer's van driver picked up the previous day's consignment and handed over six £50 notes.

So you can look at it another way: every day you spend £60 on materials, £60 on labour and £20 on overheads – making a total of £140 – and get back £300 in sales.

Hey, wait a minute! That's £160 in profit, not £80. What's happened?

What's happened is that the money-go-round is paying off. By keeping everything moving, by having five consignments of spoons in the workshop at once, including the raw materials that have just arrived and the finished goods awaiting collection, we have divided overheads by five. Each consignment only has to carry a fifth of £20, for five days' overheads, at a fifth of £20 a day.

But of course to get the pay-off, your cash has to keep moving and keep changing into different shapes: cash, raw materials, work in progress, finished goods, sales, cash, more raw materials, and so on, round and round the money-go-round.

Note: Debtors and Creditors

The money-go-round has an accelerator and a brake. Let's look at the accelerator first.

Suppose your customers are so happy with the quality and price of your teaspoons that they ask if you can supply them with tablespoons as well.

You worry for a bit about the high cost of installing a new blanking machine and a press. So you talk it over with Harry and Sharon and Bill. And it turns out that each of them has a cousin who is looking for a job on night shift.

Night shift! That's a marvellous idea! You can get double the production out of the same machines, and you won't need any more workshop space either. No extra rent. No extra rates. Just replace the teaspoon blanking and pressing dies with tablespoon blanking and pressing dies after the day shift and carry on for another eight hours, and the money-go-round will go round twice as fast: once in the daytime and once in the night-time, instead of once in the daytime and then stopping.

And then suddenly you hit a problem. You'll have to buy double the amount of metal each day. 10 kilos of two-inch strip as well as 10 kilos of one-inch strip. And you just haven't got the cash.

But there's an answer. You can speed up the money-go-round by pressing the accelerator. The accelerator is marked 'creditors'. You ask the strip metal suppliers to supply you with 10 kilos of two-inch strip every day on a month's credit. So the two-inch strip arrives at the beginning of the month, Gary, Pete and Ed turn up for night shift, the money-go-round doubles its speed, and by the time the bill for the two-inch strip comes in at the end of the month, you've sold the tablespoons and got enough cash from the sales to pay it.

What has happened, of course, is simply that the metal suppliers have lent you the money for a month. But its effect is to enable you to get the money-go-round to go faster.

The accelerator has another use as well.

Suppose the sale of tablespoons has got going and the metal manufacturer stops giving you credit. It doesn't matter now that the sales have doubled. You're back in the old routine but doing twice as well. And then a slump hits the catering industry. Your customers have to ask you for a month's credit. They become your debtors.

Horror! No money coming in for a whole month. The customers have applied the brake to your money-go-round. The brake is marked 'debtors'.

So you can try pressing the accelerator again by asking your suppliers to give you a months' credit. This time you're not making the money-go-round go faster – you're stopping it from going slower.

If you can't get credit, you'll have to find another way of getting cash on to the money-go-round: that means refuelling – increasing the working capital. Borrow from the bank. Put more of your own money in. Sell some investments. Plough back some profits.

But if you can't, then the money-go-round will slow down. You won't be able to buy so much metal. You won't be able to pay all the wages. Perhaps you'll have to cut down to four days a week working instead of five.

But overheads will stay the same – rent and rates and insurance won't come down. So you won't only sell fewer spoons – you make less profit on each consignment as well, because the overhead share will be higher. That's why the speed of the money-go-round is crucial for the health of the business.

Scroggs: Now that he understands working capital we can leave the Balance Sheet.
    I can now explain the Profit and Loss Account to him.
Carruthers: Ah! That's a different thing is it?
Scroggs: Yes. Now look at my Profit and Loss Account for one week: start with my income: I sold five lots of teaspoons at £300 a time. That brought in £1500. Income £1500. Now look at my expenses. I bought five lots of strip metal at £60 a time, so £300 went out on materials. I paid Harry and Sharon £100 each, so £200 went out on manufacturing labour. I paid Bill £100, so £100 went out on distribution

labour. I paid out £100 overhead, so I made a trading profit of £800 on the money-go-round. Then I got £20 on some cash I put on deposit and paid out £20 in interest on my loan capital. So I ended up with a net profit of £800.

Carruthers: Now I understand the Profit and Loss Account. What I do not understand is this: if she is making £800 a week profit, why is she not filthy rich?

Carruthers: He does not understand why I am not filthy rich because he does not understand what profit is.

Carruthers: I understand perfectly well what profit is. Profit is champagne and caviar and a decent tailor.

Scroggs: Profit is not champagne and caviar and a decent tailor. Profit is having a bigger business at the end of the year than you had at the beginning. Profit is what lets the business grow.

Working capital makes the business go round but it can't make it grow bigger. Not unless it makes a profit first. Suppose I want to make my exports grow.

I send catalogues to a lot of Europe's leading teaspoon buyers. I need extra money.

Then suppose I get an export order every week. I have to produce an extra consignment.

Another ten kilos of strip metal. I need extra money.

Overtime for my people. I need extra money.

Then I'll want a packing machine to help Bill cope with the extra volume. Extra money.

There's no doubt about the best place to get extra money: use the extra that came out of the working capital merry-go-round last year, and that extra is profit.

Now, the first thing that happens to profit is the tax man takes his slice of Corporation Tax. Right?

Then I and my fellow shareholders decide how much of what is left we want to put back into the business for next year's development and growth.

And the remainder, if any, we share out as dividends.

And we can spend that on caviar and cigars and a bulging wardrobe of fabulous frocks. If we want to.

Carruthers: Ah, I'd never thought of it like that.

Scroggs: Wait a moment. Remember the two places money came from. Our own money we risked, and the money we borrowed?

Carruthers: Yes.

Scroggs: Well, once the business makes a profit, there's a third place: the profit we put back into the business. It's called '**Reserves**'.

Carruthers: Ah, yes, I understand reserves. Reserves are chests full of money stashed away in a bank vault.

Scroggs: Reserves are not stashed away in a bank vault. Or not necessarily. They could be represented by machinery, or raw materials, or property.

Carruthers: Machinery? Machinery can't be Reserves.

Scroggs: Yes it can.

Carruthers: Well she's using the word in a very silly and misleading way.

Scroggs: Yes. But that's the way it's used.

Carruthers: Oh dear, oh dear! Please explain reserves very slowly.

Scroggs: Reserves is an entry in the 'In' column. It merely states where the money came from: from money retained in the business. It does not state what

the money has been used for – where it has gone to.
Carruthers: Ah, I think I am learning something new to me.
Scroggs: Some of it can go to increase fixed assets – like the packing machine for Bill. And some of it can go into working capital – like the extra strip metal and the overtime for Harry and Sharon. And some of it can be put by for a rainy day. You can invest it.
Carruthers: Or stash it in a bank vault.
Scroggs: If you're very sophisticated, yes.
Carruthers: Well now, let's see if I've got this right. Once the business has got going, there's three places you can get money from:

> your own, share capital:
> borrowing, loan capital:
> and retained profit, reserves.

And then there's three places it can go to . . . fixed assets, working capital – that's the old merry-go-round – and investments.
Scroggs: He's got it! By George, I think he's got it! Now at last we can look at a real balance sheet.
Carruthers: Well, we can look at a balance sheet but it will not get us very far because I do not understand the bit where they always talk about current assets and current liabilities.
Scroggs: Well, I see his problem. That bit is simply a snapshot of the working capital at a single moment in time:

The merry-go-round is suddenly frozen. Look, if I stop the factory working, you can see that £60 of my working capital cash has been turned into strip metal. It's just as much of an asset as cash, but in a different form. So I have £60 of assets in raw material. Then I have stamped blanks – ten kilos of strip metal with £20 of Harry's labour as well, £80, and pressed spoons, ten kilos of strip metal with £20 of Harry's labour and £20 of Sharon's. £100.

That's £180 of assets in work in progress.

Then there's a case of spoons packed by Bill and taken to the collection bay. That's £60 of strip, another £60 for three people's work – £120 – and the week's overhead of £100. That's £220 worth of assets in finished goods.

Then there's £300 I'm owed for a consignment collected last week, and £200 I put in the bank yesterday. So there's my current assets:

Raw material	60
Work in progress	180
Finished goods	220
Debtors	300
Cash at bank	200
which is . . .	£960

Take away the two bills I haven't paid yet for £60 and £100, my current liabilities, that's £160 I owe my creditors. So my net working capital at this moment is current assets of £960 less current liabilities of £160. £800.

Carruthers: I see.
Scroggs: Now we can look at the complete balance sheet again and he will explain it to me.
Carruthers: I will now explain the balance sheet to her. Well, there are only three places money can come from. Er, *Share Capital*, which is put in by the shareholders on their own risk. Er, *Loan Capital*,

which is money borrowed on a long term basis, and *Reserves*, which is profit put back into the business.

But the money is not there. It is in the business.

There are only three places in business that money can go to. Ah, *Fixed Assets* which are things you mean to keep.

Working Capital which are things you mean to sell; the money can be in raw material, work in progress, or finished goods, or in the bank, or people can owe it to you. And you subtract the money you owe other people.

And *Investments* which are savings for a rainy day, or money put in someone else's business.

Summary: Calculating Working Capital and the Profit and Loss

If your working capital keeps moving all the time, how do you ever know how much you actually have at any given moment? How do you know how much to enter in the balance sheet under 'Working Capital'?

Well, first you shout, 'STOP!'

You freeze everything at 5.30 p.m. on Friday.

And then you simply count up what you've got, in terms of the cash you have put into it.

Once the money-go-round is moving, you usually add in the overheads according to stage of completion – £20 in total per consignment, so a third of that after stamping, two-thirds after pressing, and the whole lot after packing. The following figures are expressed a little differently from those Rita used for her painstaking explanations to Julian but the principles are, of course, identical.

		£
1	10 kilos of strip metal bought today (Friday)	60.00
2	10 kilos of metal bought yesterday (Thursday) and stamped by Harry today	
	Cost of metal	60.00
	Harry's labour (1 day)	20.00
	Overheads (1/3 x £20)	6.67
		86.67
3	10 kilos of metal bought on Wednesday, stamped by Harry on Thursday, and pressed into spoons by Sharon today	
	Cost of metal	60.00
	Harry's labour (1 day)	20.00
	Sharon's labour (1 day)	20.00
	Overheads (2/3 x £20)	13.33
		113.33
4	10 kilos of metal bought on Tuesday, stamped by Harry on Wednesday, pressed into spoons by Sharon on Thursday, and packed and delivered by Bill today	
	Cost of metal	60.00
	Harry's labour (1 day)	20.00
	Sharon's labour (1 day)	20.00
	Bill's labour (1 day)	20.00
	Overheads – completed	20.00
		140.00
5	Payment received today for the consignment of spoons collected by	

Imperial Hotels Ltd 6 x £50 notes	300.00
6 Add on to this the £160 surplus on each of the previous four days, which you put into the bank. You received £300 each day and spent £60 on the next day's strip metal, paid the three workers their £20 each, and paid the day's £20 overhead: £300 – £140 = £160 x 4	640.00
7 And there's the money due from the Egg and Spoon restaurant chain who took delivery last week but always take three weeks before paying	300.00

None of this is fixed assets – it's all on the money-go-round. But it's all part of the assets. So we call these current assets. (Some people don't call cash a part of current assets – they see it as money in a transit camp which could be sent to fixed assets, current assets or investments. But for our purposes we'll call it current assets.) And we use shorter names. On the balance sheet we would put:

Working Capital

Current Assets:	£
Raw Material (1)	60
Work in progress (2 and 3)	200
Finished goods (4)	140
Cash in hand (5)	300
Cash at bank (6)	640
Debtors (7)	300
	1,640

But you can't call all that your working capital – you put an advertisement in *Catering Hardware Monthly* last month and you haven't paid the bill yet. It cost £160. And you're off on your holidays at the weekend, so you'll be taking £740 of your profits off with you this evening. Those have to be subtracted. So after current assets we put:

	£
Less Current Liabilities:	
Creditors	160
Proposed dividend	740
	900

So Net Working Capital
(Current assets less current liabilities)   740

But always remember that the business itself is never static. It's always moving. If you'd shouted 'STOP!' five minutes earlier, Imperial Hotels wouldn't have arrived with the £300, and it would all look different. Five minutes later and you would have paid out another £60 for another day's supply of strip metal, and it would all look different again. A balance sheet is a snapshot, freezing at one moment of time a perpetually moving and changing process.

But you will also want to be able to answer (as far as possible) a group of questions about the past. Where did the money come in from in the past year? What was it spent on? Did I make a profit or a loss – or to put it more accurately, did my money grow or shrink over the twelve months? Would it have grown more in a Building Society or on deposit at the bank? This group of questions is answered by the Profit and Loss Account.

The Profit and Loss Account is your history book.

And you will also want to be able to answer (as far as possible) a group of questions about the future. What is going to happen to my money in the next twelve months? Where is it going to come from? What is it going to be spent on? And – very important – when is it going to come in and when is it going to have to be paid out? Will there be enough for me to carry out my plan and carry on the business? This group of questions is answered by the Cash Flow Forecast. The Cash Flow Forecast is your crystal ball.

Let's look at the past, at the group of questions about last year. A Profit and Loss Account for your year making teaspoons could simply look like this:

		£
Sales		75,000
Less:		
Materials	15,000	
Labour	15,000	
Overheads	5,000	(35,000)
Trading Profit		40,000
Interest on investments		5,000
Net profit		45,000

And that's all there is to it. Simply take away what you spent in the twelve months from what you earned in the twelve months and the result is your profit. If you spent more than you earned, the result is your loss.

Or to put it another way, if you've made a profit there's more money on the money-go-round; your business has grown. If you make a loss there's less, and the business has shrunk. Profit is actually only a measurement of how much bigger your business has become over the past year.

Of course the Profit and Loss Account above is oversimplified. You'd probably itemise more separate expenses: selling expenses, distribution expenses, administration expenses, financial expenses, interest on loans. But you don't have to.

A Profit and Loss Account really is simple. Every householder or student runs their own Profit and Loss Account with every week's housekeeping. And that's the trouble.

It's the trouble because the Profit and Loss Account is hiding an awful lot from you. There are an awful lot of questions it isn't answering.

In a basic way, it isn't telling you how your costs relate to your sales. Suppose you've been making tablespoons as well as teaspoons. The Profit and Loss Account may be concealing the fact that you're making a loss on all your tablespoon sales, and a very big profit on all the teaspoon sales. You can find out, but you will have to ask for separate costings for each product. The Profit and Loss Account is silent about relative profitability of different lines.

It isn't even telling you how you've done on the year. Sure, it's telling you that profit is more than 50 per cent of turnover, which sounds pretty good. But suppose your Spoonmaster Blanking machine cost £3 million and your Master Cutler Press cost £2 million? In that case an investment of £5 million has brought in a return of less than 1 per cent and you'd have done far better to leave it on deposit at the bank. The Profit and Loss is silent about how much capital is invested in the business. Nor is it telling you if the business is solvent. You might have made a loss of £100,000 last year and still be £55,000 in the red. The Profit and Loss is silent about last year.

It doesn't even tell you if there's any spare cash around. You may have just bought a new workshop, freehold, for £50,000, using up all your surplus for the year and taking on a £5000 overdraft as well. The Profit and Loss is silent about what has been done with the profits.

And your two machines may be worn out and need replacing some time in the next year, at a cost of £80,000, taking all your profit and more. The Profit and Loss is silent about future expenditure commitments.

And it may be that these profits are a depressing fall from the previous year's figure, or alternatively an encouraging improvement. The Profit and Loss is silent about long term trends.

The point is that anyone can understand what a Profit and Loss is telling them.

What distinguishes the people who understand business is that they understand what the Profit and Loss Account isn't telling them.

Oh yes. There's something else we left out of the Profit and Loss Account. Everything we dealt with was a part of the working capital of the business: part of the money-go-round. We showed a profit because our current assets have grown more than our current liabilities over the past twelve months.

But has the whole business grown?

You remember that we saw from the balance sheet that there were three places we could put the company's capital. Working capital was just one. There were two others – investments and fixed assets.

Suppose you invested unwisely and the investment has

shrunk in value? Or alternatively suppose it has grown tremendously? Suppose you had invested £2000 in a piece of land, got planning permission and had it revalued at £20,000? That would bring a further £18,000 on to the profit side under the 'Revaluation of Investments'.

And what about the fixed assets? We know that the Spoonmaster Blanking Machine and the Master Cutler Press are not worth as much after being worked hard for twelve months as they were when the year began. They have shrunk in value by £2,000 each. So you reflect this by an entry of £4,000 on the loss side under 'Depreciation of Fixed Assets'.

So now we can expand the Profit and Loss Account a bit:

Profit and Loss Account

		£
Sales		75,000
Less:		
Materials	15,000	
Labour	15,000	
Overhead	5,000	
Depreciation of fixed assets	4,000	(39,000)
Trading profit		36,000
Interest on investments		5,000
Net profit realised		41,000
Unrealised surplus on revaluation of property		18,000
Total recognised gains for the year		59,000

So the complete Profit and Loss Account tells you the result of the growth or shrinkage of the total business in the past twelve months by combining the separate growth or shrinkage in the three places you can put your money: working capital (trading profit or loss), fixed assets (depreciation or revaluation or sale at profit or loss) and investments (depreciation or revaluation, or receipt of interest or dividends, or sale at profit or loss).

It's normal to distinguish what's been realised in cash (trading profit and the interest) from what's still a twinkle in the valuer's eye (the revaluation surplus) – so the Profit and Loss gives one piece of useful information. But it still doesn't answer the other unanswered questions.

Note: Depreciation and Revaluation

Let's have a look at the new Master Cutler Press. Fine piece of machinery. So it should be at £16,000.

What's more, it's got a good eight years' working life in it: it will be able to produce eight million spoons – give or take a few thousand – before it's clapped out and before the new technology brings in improved electronic calibration and controls. And better still, it's paid for. Cash on the nail. It's yours.

But just wait a minute. What do you mean 'paid for'? If it's paid for, why is it in the balance sheet at £16,000?

The fact is, it isn't paid for: at least not in the way a bar of chocolate is paid for. When you've eaten the chocolate, that's it. Gone. But the press is still there.

It's much more like your car. You bought the car, and

you can sell it again. You merely changed cash into property. It's the same with the press: you merely changed liquid assets into fixed assets. You're not any poorer, you're less liquid.

So although you've 'paid' for the press, it is not used up yet in the sense of money that's gone and can't be got back, like a bar of chocolate after you've eaten it. But it's going to be used up; because in eight years' time your Master Cutler Press is going to be worth nothing. And what happens then to the £16,000 fixed asset in the balance sheet?

What's happening, of course, is that the press is losing a little bit of its value every day you keep it and every time you use it, and in eight years it will have lost the whole £16,000. That's £2000 a year. £8 every working day. That means that a true cost of each day's output includes not just raw materials, labour and overheads, but also 1/2000th of the purchase price of the Master Cutler Press. If you turn out four thousand spoons a day, each spoon carries 1/8,000,000th of the capital cost of the press, as well as materials, labour and overheads.

That steady loss in value of fixed assets, which is known as depreciation, has to be reflected in the balance sheet each year. If the Spoonmaster cost the same as the Master Cutler and has the same length of life, then together they are depreciating at £4000 a year. Or to put it another way, every year they are taking £4000 worth of their value out of themselves and putting it into the spoons. They are another part of the cost of production – £8 a day each – and have to be reflected in the Profit and Loss Account, so that 'depreciation of fixed assets' takes place with materials, labour and overheads as part of the day-to-day cost of production.

It all sounds very straightforward; so it is. But there are two traps.

The first trap is that depreciation looks as if it's just a paper transaction. You don't actually fork out any cash, as you do for materials and wages and heating and so on. You just make a book entry, which has the effect of reducing profit. But then one day the machines actually do have to be replaced, and what's more the new technology and rising costs have doubled their price. So unless you've been depreciating the machines in the books, you can get a nasty shock.

The second trap is the profitability delusion. If you depreciate your fixed assets to nothing quite early in their life, your percentage return on capital may look unrealistically good; the reason is that you are actually using more capital than the books show, in that machines valued at zero are still actually producing. This may lead to complacency and relaxation, to be followed by an unpleasant jolt when the new machines are installed and brought into the books at cost price, and your percentage return on assets plummets.

This trap is a special danger when the fixed assets are property. Many family businesses fooled themselves that their return on assets was respectable at 15 per cent, but were only able to do so because of the large amount of freehold property they owned and valued in the books at the price Grandpa paid for it fifty years ago. These were the businesses that smart operators bought for a million on Monday, and then sold the freeholds in them for five million on Tuesday: they were – and are – an asset-stripper's dream.

So don't fool yourself that revaluation and depreciation of property and fixed assets is an accountants' game.

There may be reasons for the accountants' changing their appearance from time to time, but you must never lose sight of the reality behind the figures.

Carruthers: You see, it's all very simple. I now understand how business works.
Scroggs: He does not understand how business works because there is one thing I still haven't told him.

I will prove he does not understand by asking him whether he would accept this order.
Carruthers: Ah, now this order is from Superior Snacketerias Ltd. They want five shipments of teaspoons a week for eight weeks from the 1 April. Instead of the normal £300 a consignment they will pay £400 to compensate for taking up the entire production capacity for the eight weeks. Well, as a sophisticated manager, I can work this out. . . . £100 a day is £500 extra a week. £500 extra a week for eight weeks is . . . is . . .
Scroggs: Four thousand.
Carruthers: Four thousand. That is an extra profit of £4000. I would accept this order.
Scroggs: He hasn't read the last sentence.
Carruthers: The last sentence reads . . . 'payable in full by the 30th September'.
Scroggs: I will now introduce him to the last of the three crucial documents for understanding business finance. I have shown him the Profit and Loss

Account, which tells you what happened to your money in the past. That's your financial history book.

I have shown him the Balance Sheet, which tells you where your money is at present. That's your financial snapshot, a picture of the business frozen at a single moment of time.

I will now show him the document that tells you where your money will be going in the future. That's your financial crystal ball. It is called the Cash Flow Forecast.

But first I must ask him some more questions. How much a week will it cost to make the spoons for Superior Snacketerias?

Carruthers: Ah well, I think I can answer that. Um . . . fifty kilos of light alloy strip at £6 per kilo is £300. Next, £20 per day for each of the three people is £60 a day – that's £300 a week. Making £600 so far. And £100 overhead makes £700. It will cost £700.

Scroggs: And how much will come in each week?

Carruthers: £400 a shipment each day for five days is . . . £2000 per week.

Scroggs: But when will that £2000 actually arrive?

Carruthers: Payable in full on . . . 30 September. It will arrive in six months' time.

Scroggs: So how do we pay the people and pay the bills and buy the new lot of strip metal?

Carruthers: We . . . have some money in the bank.

Scroggs: Yes. We have £2000 in the bank.

Carruthers: Fine. We'll use that.

Scroggs: Very sophisticated! So let us look at the Cash Flow Forecast. We start week one with £2000. How much comes in in that week?

Carruthers: Nothing.
Scroggs: How much goes out?
Carruthers: £700.
Scroggs: Which leaves?
Carruthers: £1300.
Scroggs: So we start week two with . . .?
Carruthers: £1300.
Scroggs: How much cash comes in in week two?
Carruthers: Nothing.
Scroggs: How much goes out?
Carruthers: £700.
Scroggs: Which leaves?
Carruthers: £600.
Scroggs: So we start week three with . . .?
Carruthers: £600.
Scroggs: How much cash comes in in week three?
Carruthers: Nothing.
Scroggs: How much goes out?
Carruthers: £700.
Scroggs: Which leaves?
Carruthers: There is no need to go on. I can see where all this is leading because I am a sophisticated manager.
Scroggs: All this is leading to a cash deficit after eight weeks of £3600 . . . which means bankruptcy, as the consequence of accepting a profitable order.
Carruthers: I have changed my mind about accepting that order. My advice is that we should not accept it.
Scroggs: Perhaps we should not accept it. Perhaps we should negotiate weekly payments. Perhaps we should borrow some more working capital from the bank. But whatever we do, we start from a Cash Flow Forecast. There's no perhaps about that.

Carruthers: I now understand business finance. Do I?
Scroggs: Yes.
Carruthers: Yes I do. Apparently it is all about money. Money goes into investments – savings for a rainy day. It goes into Fixed Assets – things you mean to keep. And it goes into Working Capital, things you mean to sell. Working Capital starts with raw materials. It then goes into labour to produce the teaspoons – the goods. It goes into the overhead to pay the bills. Then it goes to the customer who pays you more money than you put in. The money goes round again and also you have some profit. Some of the profit goes in tax, some goes into dividends, and the rest goes to making the business grow.

I also understand that the more you produce each week, the more profit you make on each order, because you divide up the overheads into smaller portions. I even see that the less you produce each week, the less profit you make on each order because it has to carry proportionately more of the overhead.

I also understand the three crucial documents. The Profit and Loss Account tells me what has happened to my money in the past. The Balance Sheet tells me where my money is now. And the Cash Flow Forecast tells me where it will be coming from in the future.

In fact I am now ready to start my own business. You may be basic and unspoiled, but you have money. Will you come in with me?
Scroggs: I may be basic and unspoiled, but I am not stark staring sophisticated.

Summary: Cash Flow and its Importance

Balance Sheet for the present. Profit and Loss Account for the past. Cash Flow for the future.

Of course you can examine cash flow in the past as well. Indeed a Cash Flow Statement for the past twelve months will tell you some of the things that the Profit and Loss Account conceals. If, for example, you had sold £20,000 worth of investments and bought £20,000 worth of new machinery, that would not appear at all in the Profit and Loss Account. It does not affect your assets or your liabilities; it merely moves your assets into a different place. A statement of cash flow over the past twelve months, however, will show that cash has been taken out of investments and put into fixed assets.

But we're talking about the future, about the next twelve months. You want to know where you will be in twelve months' time, right? Let's say you estimate that next year's sales will be 20 per cent up on this year, and materials, labour and overheads up only 10 per cent. So at the end of next year the Profit and Loss Account would look like this:

		£
Sales		90,000
Less:		
Materials	16,500	
Labour	16,500	
Overhead	5,500	
Depreciation	4,000	(42,500)
Net Profit		47,500

(No income from investments because you spent them, and last year's profits, building a fine new brick collection bay.)

So you look like making nearly £50,000 profit this year. Fine. And then you get a real windfall. One of your regular customers, Superior Snacketerias Ltd, asks if you will do a special order. They want to restock all their cafés right across Europe with a special design of teaspoon that is exclusive to them. They want fifty kilos a week for thirteen weeks 1 April–30 June, and to compensate for taking all your production, they will pay £40 a kilo instead of the £30 you get for standard teaspoons. What's more they'll supply the pressing die to fit your Master Cutler Press. So it couldn't be easier; turn the workshop over to their teaspoons for thirteen weeks and you'll make £6500 extra profit – thirteen times the extra £100 a day, £500 a week, that Superior Snacketerias are paying for the special design.

Any snags? No, not really. See, at the bottom of the contract it says that they will pay the full sum due to you on or before 30 September. So it will all come into this year's accounts all right.

But just let's stop for a moment and think. Because if you don't stop for a moment and think now, you will have a nasty surprise some time in June. You will run out of cash.

Let's assume the first quarter goes according to plan and you make a quarter of your year's £47,500 – and after paying a dividend and some tax, you've got £7500 in the bank on 31 March.

Then you re-tool and start producing the thirteen-week run for Superior Snacketerias Ltd. Last year's costs were £140 a day, £700 a week. They've gone up 10 per cent, so let's call them £154 a day this year, £770 a week. But now that you've stopped your other work, you no longer have those six £50 notes every day to keep the money-go-round moving. (In fact, you got two lots on Fridays this year because of your 20 per cent sales increase.)

But you still have £770 a week expenses to pay.

Oh well, there's money in the bank. We'll get it all back later. A pity, in a way: that £7500 brought in £6 a week interest. It won't bring in so much now.

Indeed it won't. And next week it will bring in less. And after ten weeks it will have gone. And still no more money coming in for another three weeks and the lads to pay and the metal to buy and the bills coming in. You're broke.

Perhaps the bank will tide you over the last three weeks. Perhaps they'll lend you the expenses you'll incur. But you'll still be paying interest on it for another three months; and you'll still be losing the interest on your £7500 for another three months.

But suppose nobody lends you the money or gives you the credit? Suppose you can't get the metal, the power is cut off and the lads go and work somewhere else? Suppose Superior Snacketerias Ltd say that by only delivering ten weeks' supply instead of thirteen you've broken the contract and they're not paying?

Of course it's unlikely. But all the same it makes it worth stopping for a moment before you accept the order. And the basis of your thinking is a cash flow forecast for April to September.

	April	May	June	July	Aug	Sept
Expenditure	3,080	3,080	3,850	3,080	3,080	3,850
Income	Nil	Nil	Nil	7,200	7,200	35,000
Balance B/F	7,500	4,420	1,340	(2,510)	1,610	5,730
Balance C/F	4,420	1,340	(2,510)	1,610	5,730	36,880

A simple profit projection for the year does not show up that crisis point in June when you will not be able to pay your bills. It shows that the bus will finally reach the bank, but it does not show whether you will have enough cash in your pocket to pay the fare. Only the Cash Flow Forecast does that and it gives you the warning signal in time for you to arrange bridging finance from the bank or write progress payments into the contract. A Cash Flow Forecast, month by month or week by week, or even day by day, is the nearest thing to a crystal ball that you will get from your accountant.

It may seem surprising to some, but more businesses are wrecked on the rocks of cash flow than any other hazard, especially small and medium-sized businesses. Why?

It isn't because people can't do the sums. It's because they won't. And the reason they won't is that they do not think it is necessary. Why not? Because cash flow problems are essentially (though not universally) the problems of success.

You've landed a big order. Great news. It is signed by a cast-iron, copper-bottomed customer. You've costed it out and the profit is bound to be good and might be sensational. So why worry? If you run short you're sure the bank will lend you all you need on the strength of the customer's signature. You're laughing.

But the fact is that the expansion of work to meet an order is always going to cost money – working capital. More people to pay. More materials to stock up with. More staff work. And what is more – and this is the rub – that money is cash that has to be paid out now, and next week, and next month, but the payment only comes at the end of the job.

And the trouble about your costs is that a lot of them are people costs. The higher the people costs, the bigger the problem. You may be able to stall on the rent and the rates if you can show that there's a big order in the pipeline. You may be able to stall on the heating bills and the bank interest and the payments to suppliers. But you can't stall on wages and salaries, because they are people's housekeeping money and the children's clothes and the HP and mortgage payments.

But of course you took that into account, didn't you? In your calculations you worked out that you could take care of the costs until the payment arrived. Yes, but you were happy, euphoric and flushed with success, and you didn't take one small extra factor into account.

Vulnerability.

Once you start stretching your cash, going into debt and playing the negative cash flow game, your head is on the block, or you're walking a tightrope, or you're out on a limb. Choose your own metaphor. And things can happen – perhaps things that are not in any way your fault – that can bring down the axe, or cut the tightrope, or saw off the limb.

Try thinking of a few:

- Your sales drop off.
- Rising costs cut into your profit margin.
- Bank interest rates go up.
- You suffer production delays.
- Your suppliers are late on delivery.
- The customer lengthens the delivery date.
- The customer is late in paying.

They can all happen, and so can many others. And if more of them happen than you bargained for, they all lead to the same nightmare; the workers queuing up at the cashier's window on Friday and no cash to put in the envelopes.

That's why cash flow, and above all negative cash flow, requires a constant awareness of danger and a vigorous discipline of control.

Of course cash flow has another side to it. When Sir Jack Cohen built the Tesco Empire he did it on positive cash flow. He got his tea from Brook Bond on three months' credit but started collecting cash from the housewife on the day of delivery, when he sold it to her.

So by the time he paid for the tea, he'd got enough cash to open another store. Well, it wasn't quite that simple in detail, but that was the principle.

But even if you play it Sir Jack Cohen's way, you have to watch the cash like a hawk, because the moment sales start to drop off you're in real danger.

And if you're not playing it Sir Jack Cohen's way, you can never afford to relax or drop your guard, above all when you're expanding, and above all when you have a labour-intensive business. It's the reverse of the overheads problem: overheads are the special problem of contraction, when the business drops off but you still have to pay all the permanent staff. As with cash flow, it's the high 'people' element in overheads which causes most of the pain. The difference is that most people are acutely aware of the people problem when there's a sudden contraction of the business. The difficulty is to make them equally aware of the potential people problem when there's a sudden expansion of the business.

Note: The Business and its Accounts

---

1 Gearing

What is the business really worth?

There are two reasons why you are not going to be satisfied with the answer:

   a The question is in fact a number of separate questions.

b There is no way of giving an exact answer to any of them.

Let's look at the first reason and try to unpick the different questions.

How much is your house worth?

Well, the house two doors away sold for £120,000 last month, so let's take that as the figure.

So if you sold it, you'd come away from the deal with £120,000 in your pocket.

Ah, no. It's got a 75 per cent mortgage. Mind you, some of it has been paid off. And the mortgage was on a purchase price of £80,000 five years ago.

So you'd actually come away with about £70,000? Right? Right.

So we've already established two values for your house: the total value, £120,000, and the equity (or 'owners') value, £70,000.

The same applies to a business: its total value may include fixed assets, raw material, work in progress and stocks of finished goods which have been purchased by means of a big loan from a finance company, a socking great overdraft at the bank and a huge pile of unpaid bills. If so, the equity – the amount that is left to the owner or owners after every debt has been paid – is likely to be very small.

Or there may be no loan capital, a big cash credit in the bank, and only a trivial number of unpaid bills. In that case the value of the equity will be very close to the value of the company.

Let's stop and look at this point for a moment, because it's important. The value and the stability of any company are greatly affected by how much of the cash in the business belongs to the owners, and how much they have borrowed. Or if you prefer the jargon, the ratio of loan capital to owners' capital. It's called 'gearing', and this is why:

Suppose you had started your spoon factory on a much grander scale. You borrowed £1,000,000 from the bank at 15 per cent, and you put in just £1000 of your own. And let's suppose that you make 16 per cent overall profit on your investment in the year.

You have to pay back interest of 15 per cent, so your profit is only a teeny measly 1 per cent. But hold on a moment. One per cent of £1,001,000 is £10,010. You have made a personal profit of over £10,000 on a personal investment of £1000. An annual interest rate of more than 1000 per cent.

Fantastic! Why doesn't everyone do it?

I'll tell you why. Just suppose business had turned down in the second half of the year, and your overall return dropped 2 per cent to 14 per cent. Or suppose business stayed the same at 16 per cent, but bank interest went up 2 per cent from 15 to 17 per cent. You've now made a loss of 1 per cent – and that is a loss of £10,000, which is ten times more than you've got. You've gone bust in a very comprehensive way.

Disaster!

But suppose it was geared the other way round: 1 million of your own cash and £1000 from the bank. In that case the 2 per cent drop in business would only serve to reduce your personal profit from £160,000 to £140,000, which is still respectable. And a 2 per cent rise in interest charges adds only £20 to your year's costs.

You can think of gearing as two meshing cog-wheels.

If the loan cog-wheel is huge and the equity cog-wheel is tiny, then the gearing is high and equity can be driven round at a tremendous rate by the loan. But it can be driven in either direction: you can hurtle up to a spectacular gain or down to a spectacular loss. All very exciting but very unstable. But as the loan cog-wheel gets smaller and the equity cog-wheel gets larger, so the gearing gets lower and the excitement dies down. The loan has less and less power to move the equity value up or down to any significant degree.

So before you can have any idea of what a business is worth, you have to look at the gearing, the amount of borrowed cash it is living on. If it has no loan, then the business value and the equity value are the same. If not, you get two answers to the one question – the total value and the equity value.

2 The value of a business: valuation of assets

Let's assume it's the equity value of the business we want to establish. What is the company worth to the owner or owners?

Again, this question has two answers, because the company is likely to have two quite different values, depending on whether the owners, the shareholders, want to leave their money in the business, or to cash in their chips and stash the loot in a trunk under the bed. In other words, the company has a 'going concern' value and a 'break-up' value.

If it's the 'going concern' value you're after, then all the work in progress and stocks are worth what you paid for the raw materials plus the value you've added to them. The machines are worth what you've paid for them less the amount of value you've taken out of them.

But if it's the 'break-up' value you're after, who wants a load of blanked but unpressed teaspoons? Who wants a half-clapped-out Super Spoonmaster Blanking machine and a half-clapped-out Master Cutler Press? Once the money-go-round stops going round, everything on it is likely to lose value. (A significant exception used to be property freeholds, as we have seen – though the slump of the early 1990s took the gilt off those.)

OK. So you've refined your question 'What is the business worth?' down to something answerable: 'What is the "going concern" value of the equity?' or 'What is the break-up value of the equity?'

So now we can give you a clear and unambiguous answer?

No, we can't.

But we can now do something nearly as useful. We can show you why there can never be a clear and unambiguous answer.

Answer this question: What is a Super Spoonmaster Blanking machine worth after eighteen months?

- Harry thinks it has a ten-year lifespan so it's worth 85 per cent of its original cost.
- Sharon thinks the new technology will mean replacing it in three and a half years' time, so it's worth only 70 per cent of its original costs.
- Bill agrees with Harry about its lifespan but thinks it loses half its value in its first twelve months' operation, so it's worth less than 50 per cent of its original costs.

Or, what are the finished stocks worth?

- Harry thinks they're worth their full sale price.
- Sharon thinks the market is going soft and they can only be sold at 25 per cent discount.
- Bill thinks the market is saturated and they're only worth their scrap value.

Or what about the last six months of the lease on the workshop?

- Harry thinks the glaziers down the road would jump at it and would pay a premium to take it over.
- Sharon thinks it's overpriced and will only go at 30 per cent less than the present rental.
- Bill thinks no one will want it and the outstanding rental will have to be paid in full with nothing to set against it.

And so on.

In other words, valuation of the business is guesswork. Not pure guesswork – informed guesswork. But guesswork with a wide span of perfectly reasonable divergence as between an optimistic guesser and a pessimistic guesser. Any reputable accountant would sign up to Harry's estimates, or Sharon's, or Bill's. They are all honest, and they are all well-informed.

But the difference, over a large business, between the sum of Harry's cheerful guesses and Bill's gloomy ones, could be millions.

And there is one other valuation, though it only applies to public companies – companies whose shares are traded on the Stock Exchange. And that is the share price. That too is the valuation of the equity – if people who buy and sell shares think the company is worth £2 million, and you started up by issuing a million shares say, then the £1 shares are worth £2 each. You have a 'market capitalisation' of £2 million.

The market price is exactly what it says – the price in the market place. Something between the price no one would dream of buying the shares for and the price no one would dream of selling them for.

But of course the market price is not based simply on the current value of the assets. It is tremendously influenced by what people think the shares are likely to earn in the future. If you are in a suddenly booming industry, or keep improving your profits year by year, or own freehold land in a place where they've discovered oil, you could find yourself with a market capitalisation well above even Harry's optimistic valuation of the assets.

Or if you're in a slump, or someone has discovered your product damages the environment, it may easily be well below even Bill's dismal estimate.

So to sum up the value of a company; high gearing affects the value in two ways – by making the whole enterprise more risky, and by making you take a large loan sum off the total value to discover the equity value.

The equity value can be a 'going concern' value or 'break-up' value. Either valuation is subject to wide but perfectly legitimate fluctuation depending on the view you take.

And there is also the market value – the amount investors are prepared to pay for the company.

How much they offer to pay will depend on their level of strategic interest, their pessimism or optimism.

3 The profit of a business

If you think that profits are something to do with champagne and caviar and yachts in the Mediterranean, you will never understand business.

Champagne and caviar and yachts in the Mediterranean are to do with cash. You can get cash from winning the Pools, robbing banks, topping the pop charts or inheriting your rich uncle's fortune. Or from wages, salaries, interest, dividends or sales of shares.

Dividends come out of profits: but there is no necessity to pay a dividend. If you do pay one you will pay it in cash, and it will help pay for the caviar and champagne and yachts.

But profit won't.

Suppose you had a tough year in the teaspoon business. But you kept going and managed to break even. Your Profit and Loss Account shows that costs exactly equalled income, without a penny to spare. You are solvent, just, but you have no profit at all.

No profit, that is, on your working capital.

But you could still have made £20,000 profit. How? By selling for £50,000 a plot of land you had bought for £30,000. That would be profit on capital account (profit on investments) even if your trading operation brought you no profit on current account (profit on working capital).

The fact is that there are several ways of making a profit, and several places you can apply it. But you have to make a profit.

Why? Why can't you aim to break even? Obviously you don't want to make an actual loss, since that means a shrinkage of the business until it finally disappears. But why do you have to make a profit?

Well, let's look at some basic reasons.

You may want to increase your fixed assets – buy another machine, for instance. And if you're not making any profit, if every bit of cash that comes in has to go out again to pay the bills, you won't be able to. If you want to pay the extra, you have to earn extra: you have to make a profit.

You may only want to replace the Super Spoonmaster because it's worn out. And you may have set aside each year, for eight years, one eighth of its cost. You bought it for £16,000, you depreciated it by £2000 a year, and you invested that £2000 ready for replacement. But what's happened? Inflation over five years, and technological advance, have raised the latest (Mark II) Super Spoonmaster to £25,000. Where are you going to find the extra £9000, if not out of profit?

In other words, expanding the business in any way, and even merely keeping it up to date technically, requires profit. Even if you work night shifts and need no extra fixed assets, you will need extra working capital for the extra raw material and labour bills.

If inflation puts up the cost of strip metal, you'll have to find extra to pay it. You'd get it back eventually from increased prices, no doubt, but you need the extra now and the returns come later. You have to find cash to pay the night shift too, before you can sell what they produce.

Or suppose your gearing is getting dangerously high and you want to pay back some of what you have borrowed? To replace loan capital with share capital you need profits.

Or suppose you see big new expenses coming up next year – a rent review which is bound to double your rent – you want some cash saved up in advance to provide for it. That means profit.

Or suppose you have strong reasons to believe you could find a lot of new customers in France and Germany if you paid a visit and did some market research? You have to have some extra to pay the fare and hotel bills and the research costs.

Or suppose you have a marvellous idea for a double-ended teaspoon, so that people can stir the cup without wetting that part that goes back into the sugar? You'll need to produce a few and try them out on customers. But that will take extra, and the 'extra' is past profit.

All new research, investigation, development and testing have to come out of previous profit, because if every penny that comes back from customers goes out again in materials, labour and overhead, there's no cash to fund it. Of course it's a cost you can set against earnings, for tax purposes, but you've got to fund it first. Later on you can make it a permanent feature of the business, build it into the money-go-round, add it to the price of your teaspoons, and call it a cost. But if you ever want to expand research, development, marketing or sales again, you'll need more profit again.

All these uses of profit are different forms of investment in the only three areas you can put money: investments (your savings to meet the increased rent), fixed assets (renewed or additional machines) and working capital (material, labour, research, development, sales, marketing). And all new investment has to come out of the only three places you can get your money from: equity, loan or retained profit.

Of course you could have financed all the above projects with cash from one of the other two sources. You could have borrowed, but you can't go on borrowing for ever, and every borrowing saddles you with interest charges and diminishes the stability of the business. And if you're not making a profit, it gets harder and harder to borrow.

Or you could have raised new equity capital – put more of your own money into the business. But without a prospect of profit, of the money growing, you will only raise cash from certifiable idiots. And they don't have much.

So you have to have profits. And in fact the bulk of UK investment is financed from retained earnings.

But, of course, if things go right there is a pay-off every year.

The new investment last year brings in more profit this year. So let's say you make £20,000 profit – £20,000 clear after paying all your bills. And let's say it's all trading profit – no gains in capital value of investments, fixed assets or property.

The first thing that happens to that profit is that you pay tax on it. Corporation tax is payable on profit before you reinvest. Money you plough back into the business is taxed money – money that is left over after corporation tax has been paid.

The second thing that happens is you decide how much to reinvest in the three available areas – outside investment, fixed assets and working capital. All that is called transfer to reserves.

The third thing that happens is you pay yourself a dividend.

No law says you have to pay yourself a dividend. In

fact you may prefer to build up the capital value of the business by reinvesting everything that's left over after tax. If it's your own private, solely owned company you may well be advised to do so.

But suppose a hundred of you clubbed together to put up the money and so the company belongs to a hundred of you. Some may want all the after-tax profit as dividend, some may want it all ploughed back. So you elect four people to decide what is best for the hundred of you as a group. They are the Board of Directors. The chances are they decide to pay some out as dividend and keep some back to finance next year's renewal and expansion.

It's rather like farming – if you eat all the potatoes you have none to plant for next year. If you plant them all, you go hungry this year.

It is really quite unimportant where you draw the line, because your wealth increases either way: if you take a tiny percentage in dividend, your share value grows because of the huge percentage you reinvest; and if you take a huge percentage in dividend your share value diminishes, or fails to grow or grows by a much smaller amount, because of the tiny percentage you reinvest.

If you want your champagne and caviar, you can buy them out of dividends, if you distribute a lot, or by selling shares, if you reinvest a lot. They still taste the same. But either way you can only have them if the business grows. And there is only one way a business can grow, and that is by making a profit.

4 Published accounts

'You make it all sound very simple, but it's not really like that, is it?' You hold up a copy of Universal International plc's annual report and accounts as evidence. Pages and pages of small print with the occasional glossy picture of the chairman for light relief. It seems a long way from the two basic questions – where the money came in from, and where it went out to.

The trouble is that Universal International plc doesn't just make teaspoons. It has hundreds of different operations in different countries, making and selling different products in different currencies. The annual accounts are an attempt to boil it all down into the answer to the two basic questions – but all the extra information is needed by analysts to answer all the other questions, the ones about risk, trends, performance.

There are other problems with published accounts. Companies make takeover bids using the strength of their share price, so unscrupulous directors have been known to try to boost the company up a bit with 'creative accounting'. So the government, the Stock Exchange and the accountants have made rules for the minimum contents and the required layout of accounts. More detail, more jargon. But more information for those who know where to look for the warning signs.

If you look through those accounts, you'll find a balance sheet. It will have 'where the money is invested' at the top (fixed assets, current assets, current liabilities) – but at the moment, companies have to show the loan capital as a deduction from the assets instead of treating it like share capital. So the top part of the balance sheet comes down to 'net assets' – what the shareholders own.

Underneath that, you'll see the share capital and reserves. These might be a bit more complicated than the figures for Scroggs Manufacturing – but they have different ways of making profits or raising money, so there are different categories of reserves. They're all the same – something which has been retained from previous years so it can be invested in the assets in the other half of the balance sheet.

You'll recognise the profit and loss account. This gives a lot of information – for example, it splits up the results of last year between 'continuing operations' and 'discontinued operations', to give a clue about what might happen in the future. But it's still the history book of the business – what the money did in the last year.

What about the future? Well, you'll find a cash flow statement, but it isn't a cash flow forecast. It's history, like the profit and loss account. Companies don't like to publish specific forecasts about the future – people might expect them to do what they say! Also they could give away important information to their competitors if they provided too many details about their plans. So the accounts don't talk about the future – perhaps something in the chairman's statement about prospects for the business, but it'll be vague enough to fit any outcome.

So what's the cash flow statement for? We've already got a profit and loss account, why confuse us with another version of the history? The point is that, as we have seen, you can't pay your bills with profits. You need cash. If all the cash generated by profits has been absorbed in replacing the fixed assets – or if the profits are on paper only, and the company hasn't collected any of its debts – then you would see it in the cash flow statement. It answers some of the questions which the profit and loss account doesn't.

All right, published accounts are complicated. They have to be because businesses are complicated. There have to be rules to deal with directors who are over-optimistic or downright dishonest. There has to be extra information for the analysts and financial journalists, as well as the basic stuff which the ordinary shareholder wants to know. But you'll probably understand a surprising amount if you keep your eyes on the basic questions – Where did the money come from? Where is it now? What's going to happen to it in the future?

5 The rules of the game

'Profit, dividends, growth, assets, capital' – is that all you can think of? Is your mind so narrow and your heart so cold and hard that you see a business only in terms of figures on a balance sheet and entries in a ledger? Well, I've got news for you, Scrooge, and news for the soulless, faceless team of desiccated calculating machines computing away in your ivory tower block. You won't believe it, and you probably won't even understand it, but it is true all the same.

There is more to a business than money!

You may think that business is just a cash processing plant, turning cash into more cash. Well, Scrooge, I am here to tell you that a business is people. It engages the hopes and fears, the care, the concern and the pride of a whole community of men and women. It is a web of rivalries and loyalties, of anger and laughter, of loves and hates.

And I'll tell you something else. It can be very sweet, or it can turn very sour. The same community of people can work together with fun and fellowship, with commitment and co-operation, or they can seethe with bitterness and resentment and strife. And in that volatile, explosive mixture of egos and emotions there are just a few people whose job is to keep everyone working together effectively and productively. They need humour, courage, energy, enthusiasm, commitment, skill, knowledge, intelligence, experience and endless patience. They are called managers. And without them, your precious cash processing plant would seize up.

And these managers are quite busy enough organising, motivating and controlling this turbulent human community, without locking themselves up in little offices with calculators and accounts clerks and reams of paper. All you see from up there in the clouds is Budgets and Balance Sheets and Profit and Loss Accounts and Cash Flow Forecasts, and you think they will tell you what is going on. But they don't, Scrooge. They don't tell you a tenth of it!

When managers say that, how can you prove they're wrong?

You can't. Because they're right.

Financial management may be everything to the Financial Director, but if it's everything to the Line Manager you'd better sack them quick, before they have time to screw up the entire company.

The answer is quite simple. You can just as easily tell the Doctor that there is a lot more to life than systolic and diastolic blood pressure and cholesterol level and red corpuscle count. And you're right.

But if the blood stops going round you die.

And if the cash stops going round you go out of business.

Those are the rules of the game.

There's a great deal more to success in a game than keeping the rules. But if you don't keep the rules, you're out.

The rules of the game

You may be marvellous at inspiring and organising people, and at winning their affection and loyalty and trust. But if you don't keep the rules, the time will come when there's no cash to pay them with at the end of the week, and that will have a serious effect on their affection and loyalty and trust.

There's no such thing as a top class golfer who doesn't understand the rules or the scoring system, though some quite good club players get by despite being a little vague. And there's no such thing as a top class manager who doesn't understand finance, though some quite good middle and lower managers get by despite being a little vague.

You can watch a powerful, erratic golfer with a lovely free swing and a long drive play against an unexciting, awkward opponent who drives straight but short, but who is very accurate at pitching and putting. The powerful erratic player loses. Their style may be far superior, but they get knocked out and it's the boring, accurate pitch-and-putt merchant who goes on into the next round. That's what the rules say.

The finance of a business isn't all of it, or even the half of it. If all you understand is figures, you won't get very far. But finance is the scoring system and the rules of the game. And unless you understand the scoring system and keep to the rules, you're out.

Golden rules

1 Remember the three documents which depict your business: the Profit and Loss Account for the past, the Balance Sheet for the present, and the Cash Flow Forecast for the future.
2 Don't let accountancy jargon prevent you from knowing your business. Learn the basic language and understand its uses.
3 Working capital is money at work. Learn where yours is in detail and make sure it is not lying idle.
4 Profitable companies can go bust if they can't pay their bills. Never confuse profitability with liquidity.
5 Profit is not champagne and cigars. It is a measure of growth or contraction of a business.

2 The control of working capital

Working capital is the key to the profitability of every business. And the control of working capital is the heart of business management.

Money put into fixed assets and investments is the consequence of a single decision – shall we or shall we not buy this property, these shares, this machine tool? The decision may be right or wrong, but once it has been taken and the cheque has been signed, that is that.

But money put into working capital, on the money-go-round, is quite different. It is permanently under the control of the managers and workers. And there is something else about working capital: more money invested in it does not necessarily get you more of anything. Money invested in loans or shares will earn more interest or dividends, but money invested in working capital may produce absolutely nothing at all, or at least nothing of any value. It may just be swallowed up without a trace.

The control of working capital means, in effect **keeping the money tied up in working capital down to the absolute minimum level necessary to produce the sales and profits.** It means getting the best possible value, in terms of profitable sales, for every pound invested in working capital.

> **Carruthers:** Twelve months ago I was a sophisticated corporate executive. Then a certain female spoon

manufacturer purported to explain to me how business works. As a result I gave up my sophisticated position and set up a fork-manufacturing business. I am now hounded hourly by my customers, my salesmen and my bank manager, and I am living on barbiturates, tranquillisers and ulcer pills.

Scroggs: I admit that is not very sophisticated, but why are you blaming me?

Carruthers: This charlatan persuaded me that business finance is a sort of cash merry-go-round. You start with a pile of cash. You put in some of the cash and get raw materials. You put in more of the cash to pay the lads for processing the raw materials into finished goods. You put in more of the cash to pay the overheads. The customer collects the goods and hands over his cash. And you use that cash to start all over again.

Scroggs: I told you that because it is true.

Carruthers: It may be true in the spoon business, but it is not true in the fork business. In the fork business you start with a pile of cash, and you put in some for materials, some for labour and some for overheads. But no forks come out. So you borrow more cash and spend it on more materials, more labour and more overheads, on and on, until finally the forks emerge and the customer collects them. But do you get the cash then? Oh no. He just leaves a piece of paper. So you borrow even more money at appalling interest rates until at last he pays up and you get some cash to put back into the merry-go-round. But by then you're in debt up to your eyeballs.

If you like, you can think of working capital as all the money you would have to pay out in your first week as a spoon manufacturer. For a week you'd have to buy ten kilos of strip metal every day, and at the end of the week you'd have to pay the lads and pay the bills, with no money coming in at all. In other words, that's £700 out, and nothing in. That is the initial investment in working capital. After that, you might sell a consignment every day and produce a consignment every day, and clear £800 a week. But you'd never stop having that £700 of dead money going through the factory. If we looked around the workshop after the lads had gone home on Friday evening, we'd still see it there; the strip on the

Dead money

shelf, the blanks in the workshop, the spoons in the packing room, the packed crates in the collection bay, the unpaid invoices in the file – £700 of working capital. It's there because of the time factor, because you have to buy your strip metal a week before you sell it as teaspoons. It's the physical, financial, visible expression of lead-time, or time-lag, or the delay factor, or whatever else you like to call it.

But suppose it took two weeks instead of one to turn the cash spent on materials, labour and overheads back into cash received from the customer? Suppose you had taken a fortnight instead of a week when you first started the business, a fortnight of buying ten kilos of strip a day and a fortnight of wages and bills before you started selling a consignment of spoons a day? Then you'd have £1400 tied up in working capital, and not a penny more to show for it. And if you had taken a month you would have had £2800 tied up. And so on. A lot of people say time is money, but for the simple literal truth of the phrase there is no example to touch working capital.

Working capital, in fact, rests on the simple **time equals money** equation. If you increase the time it takes to produce sales revenue, you increase the working capital locked up in the business. If you can reduce the time, you liberate the capital for other purposes – which is what the control of working capital is all about.

But as Carruthers points out, in the fork business even if you do produce the goods quickly, customers do not pay up on time.

> **Scroggs:** You are quite right that customers do not always cough up.
> **Carruthers:** Then why didn't you tell me that?

Scroggs: I didn't tell you because you are so sophisticated that you can only take in one idea at a time. Then you have to have a business lunch to recover. But the solution is very simple, luckily for you – *you* don't have to cough up either. It is quite true that when you make the sale, you don't always get cash at once. That's why there is a 'debtor' button. You often have to keep pressing your debtors till you get the cash. But there is also a 'creditors' button – your creditors give you supplies without your having to pay cash. So you keep the merry-go-round turning on credit till your debtors pay you and you can pay your creditors. The two balance out. In fact, if you conduct your business really craftily you can get cash back from the customer before you pay your suppliers.
Carruthers: What you are saying is that I should keep pestering my customers for money while not paying my own bills until the last possible moment.
Scroggs: That is a crude and blunt way of putting it. But then I am a crude and blunt lady.
Carruthers: I should like to point out that I had an expensive education. I was taught never to get into debt and never to pester people for money.
Scroggs: It was an even more expensive education than you realise. You're still paying for it.
Carruthers: Very well. You have explained that the 'sale' button does not always produce cash, and that you have the pressed the 'payment' button. You have also explained that the 'credit' button can keep the money-go-round moving for a time without cash. And you have explained that the two delays should balance out. But that is only a small part of my problem. It is not the real reason for my ulcers, my

insomnia or my continual suppressed anxiety. The real reason is that I have just experienced a business disaster: my company has become successful.
Scroggs: Yes. With sophisticated people, success is normally disastrous. Immediate failure cuts their losses.
Carruthers: I was so disastrously successful that demand for my forks doubled.
Scroggs: By an extraordinary coincidence the demand for spoons also doubled, but that did not cause me any sleepless nights. It caused me great contentment. I took the extra orders, borrowed more working capital, took on more staff, ordered more strip metal, and increased my turnover and also my profit by 100 per cent. Why haven't you done the same?
Carruthers: Because I have no money. I have taken the extra orders, bought some extra metal and taken on some extra staff. But the bank will not allow me one penny of extra money. So my cheques are bouncing, my customers are shouting, my salesmen are cursing and my bank is foreclosing.

Bankruptcy through success? Yes, of course. This can happen in several ways, the most obvious being that you simply can't afford to finance the extra volume required to meet that 'successful' order. You almost certainly won't if you don't plan how to raise the necessary money and ensure that your financial commitments are not incurred long before the revenue from sales starts to come in. Then there is the problem of company costs – of course they are likely to rise to meet an expansion of business, but by how much? It is all too easy to gear yourself to expansion by increasing costs to a level which, in effect, makes the extra business unprofitable. And, of course, if the success is a 'one-off' order will those costs then go away? If you lease a new warehouse, increase the workforce – indeed add to the fixed costs in any way – you must realise that expenditure which goes on for 365 days a year is not likely to be beneficial if it equips you for orders you have now, but may well not duplicate in the future. Let's see how Scroggs has coped with success while Carruthers has not:

> **Scroggs:** I buy five consignments of strip metal a week for £500. One a day at £100 each. I pay Harry and Sharon and Bill £200 a week each – £600. My overheads come to £300 a week. Total costs of labour, materials and overheads – £1400. And I sell five consignments of spoons a week at £400 each – £2000. So I clear £600 a week.
> **Carruthers:** I too buy five consignments of strip a week for £500. I pay Ted and Jack and Gus £200 a week each. My overheads also come to £300 a week. Total also £1400. And I sell five consignments a week at £400 each – £2000. So I too clear £600 a week.
> **Scroggs:** We both pay out the same amount and get in the same amount. Why don't you borrow more from the bank, like I've done? I'm allowed to borrow up to £10,000 working capital.
> **Carruthers:** So am I. Unfortunately I have already borrowed £12,000.
> **Scroggs:** £12,000! How have you managed to get through £12,000 of working capital?
> **Carruthers:** How much have you borrowed?
> **Scroggs:** £1200.

Carruthers: £1200! How on earth do you manage on £1200 of working capital?

Scroggs: I can show you my £1200 of working capital. It is in my factory now. Look. There's the roll of light alloy strip that Harry collected this morning – £100. There's a roll of strip he stamped into blanks yesterday. That's £140 – £100 worth of light alloy and £40 worth of labour. There's a roll of strip he stamped into blanks and Sharon pressed into spoons. That's £180 – the strip and two days' labour. There's a case of finished spoons packed by Bill. That's £220 – the strip and three days' labour. And there's a case labelled and documented and ready for collection. Strip plus four days' labour – £260. And add the week's overhead of £300 on to that, and there you are. Total – £1200 tied up in working capital.

Carruthers: £1200. So this is how the other half lives.

Scroggs: My business is efficient and profitable and I am not short of cash to expand production.

Carruthers: I may have run out of cash but at least I run my business decently.

Scroggs: And use ten times as much working capital as me for the same turnover.

Everybody in an organisation is responsible, in one way or another, for keeping working capital as low as possible – in other words for turning cash paid for materials, labour and overheads back into cash received from customers as fast as possible. But there are four key areas in a business where this process is most often delayed and where working capital can be allowed to build up to unnecessary levels if it is not permanently monitored and stringently controlled.

Those four key areas are:

1 purchasing
2 production
3 finished goods
4 credit control

These are the main areas where working capital tends to pile up unnecessarily: stacks of raw materials in stores, stacks of work in progress in the workshop, stacks of finished goods in the warehouse, stacks of unpaid invoices in the office. And that's how you reach one of the classic business crises – the **overtrading crisis**. Customers are clamouring for goods, which leads to your stepping up production to meet the demand, running out of money to finance expanded production (in other words running out of working capital), suppliers and landlords clamouring for payment, the bank refusing any more loans, finance houses foreclosing, bailiffs and receivers moving in – and all because your product was so successful you just ran out of working capital.

And yet you didn't run out of working capital. It was there all the time. You just couldn't get at it. You had lots of working capital – lots of raw materials (the wrong materials), lots of work in progress (the wrong work), lots of finished goods (the wrong goods), a pile of unpaid invoices . . . stacks of working capital all tied up, locked up and dead.

These areas are hard enough to control even when everyone in the business is trying hard to control them. But there is a terrible pitfall, and it causes one of the central problems of management; the pitfall is that the people in control of these four areas can, and do, vastly increase the amount of working capital employed, and they increase it for worthy and conscientious reasons. They are often skilled, experienced, hard-working people and their motive is to keep everyone happy. The cost of keeping everyone happy, however, can ultimately destroy a company.

> **Carruthers:** My business is based on four wonderful people. They're all from the same family – the Squirrel family. The first wonderful person is my buyer, Ted Squirrel. If anyone in the workshop wants anything, Ted's got it. No waiting. Every shape and size and weight. You name it, he's got it on the shelf. That takes care of £600. Wonderful chap, Ted. Keeps everyone happy.
>
> The next wonderful person is my production manager, Jack Squirrel. Always oblige anyone. He'll even take half-finished jobs off the machine for rush orders. Finishes them off a couple of weeks later, if necessary. Always has lots of finished forks along the gangway, so if Sales start screaming he can give 'em something to shut 'em up. Keeps everyone happy, Jack. That's £840 in the stamping section and £1080 in the pressing section.
>
> My third wonderful person is my sales manager, Gus Squirrel. Looks after packing and dispatch. Terrific spare stocks of everything. And it was Gus who made us expand our range from 3 kinds of forks to 176 kinds to meet every requirement. Always oblige a customer with a rush order. Breaks into crates for non-standard quantities. Wonderful chap, keeps all the customers happy. That's £1320 for forks waiting to be packed, and £1560 for finished consignments waiting for someone to order them. Oh

yes, and overheads. Well of course it takes longer for things to go through a sophisticated system like mine; about six weeks. That's £1800 overheads.

And finally there's my fourth wonderful person. My credit controller, Gladys Squirrel. Heart of gold.
Scroggs: She'll have to go.
Carruthers: What?
Scroggs: I know the heart-of-gold type. Unpaid customer accounts going back to World War One. But the suppliers' bills get paid the day they arrive.
Carruthers: She keeps everybody happy.
Scroggs: Delirious. I should think.
Carruthers: Wonderful girl, Gladys. Debtors, £4800. Total £12,000 tied up in working capital. I have a feeling you don't think my four wonderful people are so frightfully wonderful.
Scroggs: On the contrary, they fill me with wonder *and* fright. Fortunately *my* four people try to save money and keep the company in business, instead of spending it to buy easy popularity. They believe in using as little working capital as they can, and getting the money back as fast as possible. If they didn't they'd be working for someone else. You, probably.

Take my buyer, Harry. He hates to see money lying idle on the shelves, so he doesn't buy *any* raw materials until *just* before Sharon needs them. Sharon in production whips stuff through her workshop and out again as though it was a time bomb. Bill, the sales manager, reckons every crate in the delivery bay is a mark of shame. So he rushes them out to customers the second they're packed, and rushes the dispatch notes up to Prue. And Prue in accounts gets them off as though they were telegrams. And she's marvellous at persuading suppliers to give her an extra few weeks' credit.

Once cash has been turned into goods, all my four people hustle it through the system to turn it back into cash again. Everything moves so fast that there's only £1200 in the pipeline before cash comes back from the customers to top it up again.

Carruthers: What an awful company. I would give a great deal not to have to work with people like that.

Scroggs: You are giving a great deal. You are giving £10,800, your sleep, your health and your solvency.

Yes, four wonderful people, and four effective ones. It may be a cliché that everyone in a company is 'on the same side' but you have to make sure that they all know what side that is. The first duty of a company is to stay in business, and that does not mean that everyone's interests are to be served at the expense of your firm's solvency. It does mean teaching all your staff exactly what is involved in the way they work, how it helps and how it hinders your prime objectives. Then, and only then, can your staff become both wonderful *and* effective.

But will a more realistic attitude by your staff have an adverse effect on your customers?

Carruthers: You're ignoring a vital point – I am not the only fork manufacturer in the world – I have to be competitive, at all costs.

Scroggs: You're right to say that you must compete – but *not* at all costs. £12,000 tied up in working capital is too great a cost.

Carruthers: Why is it too great a cost? All right, I'm using £12,000 working capital, while you are using

only £1200. But if I wasn't, the interest would only be a trifling 10 per cent and wouldn't solve any of my problems, so the point is irrelevant.
Scroggs: If it's irrelevant, why are you a gibbering wreck while I'm a fat cat?
Carruthers: Only because of my success.
Scroggs: The point is that having too much money tied up in working capital is not irrelevant. It is the heart of the problem. Listen. You told me last year you cleared £30,000.
Carruthers: Yes.
Scroggs: And this year business has doubled?
Carruthers: Yes.
Scroggs: Then why don't you double your production and clear an extra £30,000 this year?
Carruthers: I've told you – it would need another £12,000 of working capital. I cannot lay my hands on £12,000 of working capital. I have reached my borrowing limit.
Scroggs: So if you *could* lay your hands on another £12,000 you would not invest it at a trifling 10 per cent, you would use it to double production and make yourself another £30,000 a year profit.
Carruthers: . . . Yes.
Scroggs: You see, I only had £1200 tied up in working capital. When my business doubled, I only needed another £1200 to double production. With that £1200 I doubled my purchases of raw martials, took on my staff and worked a night shift as well as a day shift. They produced double the spoons and double the profits. I will now show you how you can do the same without borrowing another penny from the bank.

Carruthers: Either you're about to deceive me once again, or I shall be glad I came here after all.

Scroggs: Those four wonderful people of yours are actually wonderful jailers – they are keeping all your money locked up. But just suppose they released half of it. Suppose Ted started using up what's in his store before buying new stocks. Suppose Jack completed all the unfinished jobs and let the stuff out of the workshop. Suppose Gus made up his consignments *and* sold off his spare stocks. And suppose Gladys started collecting all the money from the debtors. If they could only get half your working capital out of the factory gates as forks and back in through the letterbox as cash. Imagine that!

Carruthers: It is not very sophisticated to imagine things.

Scroggs: Look. You would save half your working capital, £6000. Then you could use that to double production.

Carruthers: It's like talking to a brick wall. I explained to you that I need £12,000, and you come up with £6000.

What Carruthers still hasn't grasped is that once he has managed to cut his working capital by half, all that will have changed.

Scroggs: You will no longer need £12,000 worth of working capital – you will only need £6000 worth. So the released £6000 will be enough to double your raw material purchase, double your staff, and work night shifts as well as day shifts. Then you can double the forks and double the profits.

Carruthers: No, no, no. This is a trick.
Scroggs: It is not a trick. You do not need £12,000 in working capital. I don't believe that you need £6000, but you certainly don't need £12,000. The answer is this. All you have to do if you want to save money is to save time. If you want to run your factory on half the money, all you have to do is run it on half the time.
Carruthers: Half the time?
Scroggs: Yes.
Carruthers: Well, I know time is money. Everyone says so. My wife told me so yesterday at breakfast. I'm sure it's true, but convince me.
Scroggs: I will convince you. Let's take two imaginary people. One short, quick, poor man and one tall, slow, rich man. They both want to start up in the knife-making business. Look at the short man first. He rents a fully equipped knife factory, paying rent monthly in arrears. He gets a month's credit for his raw materials, he takes on monthly paid staff and he pays his overheads monthly. Right. He's got no money, but he's got time – one month. So he moves before his time runs out. He stamps the strip, processes the blanks, packs the crates, sells the knives and collects the cash as fast as he can. By the end of the month he can pay all the bills, order more strip, start all over again and have a bit over as well. And he's never touched his own money.

Now look at the tall, slow man.
Carruthers: I can see what's coming . . .
Scroggs: He pays rent in advance, he pays for his materials on delivery, he pays his staff weekly. And he puts the Chipmunk family in charge. Ted

Chipmunk keeps on buying more and more materials. A roll of strip spends a month on the shelf before going through to the factory. Jack Chipmunk keeps the workshop stuffed with finished and half-finished jobs, and that strip then spends a month in the factory before it comes out as knives. Gus Chipmunk keeps the collection bay full of crates, so the same strip spends a month in the crate before the customer collects it. And Gladys Chipmunk doesn't type the invoices till the end of the month, and then mails them second class. It's another three months before the cash paid for the first roll of strip comes back from the customer.

So that's where all the money went. It went in time. Six months' rent. Six months' stock of materials. Six months' wages. Six months' overheads. All before a penny came back. And that delay is now built into the system. The materials bought today will be on Ted's shelf for a month. Then it will be in Jack's workshop for a month. Then it will be in Gus's crates for a month. Then the customer won't pay for three months.

And all that tall, slow, rich man has to do to cut his working capital by half is to cut the time by half. Get Ted to carry the stocks for half as long. Get Jack to keep it in his workshop for half as long. Get Gus to send the crates off to customers with half the delay. Get Gladys to get the cash back from customers in half the time. Output will be the same. Turnover will be the same. But he will now need only half the old working capital to do the same business. That is why a certain person can manage on £6000 of working capital if he wants to.

Cash on the nail

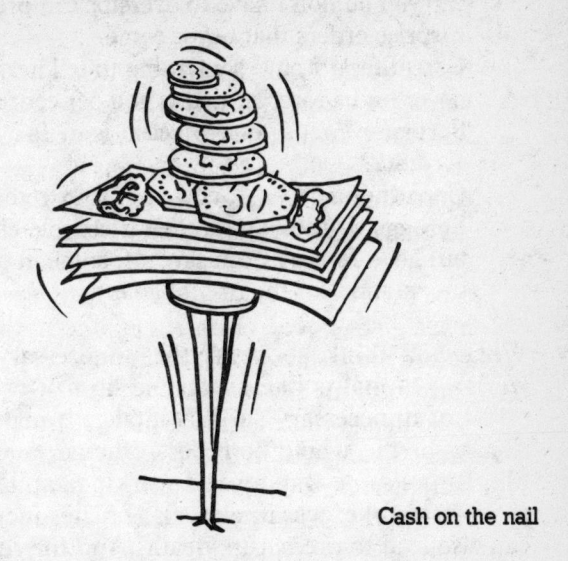

Carruthers: You may think your disguised character fooled me, but I am too sophisticated for you. I could see that you were talking about me. You were hinting that if my four wonderful people kept things for half the time they do now, I could manage on half the money.
Scroggs: That is what I was hinting.
Carruthers: But it's no good. My wonderful people would not take the risk of not keeping everyone happy.
Scroggs: You *can* keep everyone happy.
Carruthers: How?
Scroggs: Just follow two Golden Rules. Golden Rule number one is **sales forecasting**. If you have accurate sales forecasts you know what stocks you need to

carry. You don't have to overstock in preparation for surprise orders that never come.
Carruthers: I have something to tell her. She will never find a forecast that is 100 per cent accurate.
Scroggs: That's your forecast, is it? Is it 100 per cent accurate?
Carruthers: Yes . . . no . . . it is extremely accurate.
Scroggs: Quite. No forecast is completely accurate, but good forecasts can save a fortune in unnecessary preparation for the improbable.

When you think about it, the unnecessary stacked-up working capital is like fat on the human body. It is the result of unnecessary surplus intake, it makes the functioning of the whole body less efficient and it shortens life. In the same way, excess working capital also represents wasteful excess intake, also creates inefficiency and can also lead to premature death. And the reason for it is the same too – if nobody knows where the next order is coming from, for what product or in what quantity or by what date, then all you can do is put on a lot of fat and hope it will see you through. And when you think about it, nearly all those extra stocks are the consequence of uncertainty about future demand.

But modern industrial man does not need fat, because he knows where the next order is coming from. Or rather, he can get a very good idea, within top and bottom limits, of the likely volume and pattern of future orders. What it needs is sales forecasting, and sales forecasting is at the heart of the control of working capital. So the first step in the control of working capital is to produce accurate sales forecasts, to keep them constantly under review, and to revise them quickly as soon as change becomes apparent. So the first of the two Golden Rules is to get the fastest and most trustworthy sales forecasting system you can.

> **Scroggs:** Golden Rule number two is to have **regular meetings** to see how you can bring down the working capital and keep it down.

These meetings will involve at least the people responsible for buying, manufacturing, selling and payment collection.

Such meetings have a single purpose, to work out all possible ways of shortening the time between paying money to suppliers and collecting it from customers.

More meetings? Yes. If the buyer alone decides what stocks to delay buying he may be sabotaging the production manager. If the production manager makes a decision about changing the manufacturing programme he may leave the buyer with surplus stocks and the sales manager short of goods. And so on. When the whole team get together they may come up with suggestions for speeding up the money-go-round: the home sales manager may be perfectly happy to promote a different line in order to help run down the excess stocks that resulted from a cancelled export order, or the credit controller may get the dispatch manager to get Friday's dispatch notes to the office before lunch so that invoices can go out on Friday afternoon instead of Monday morning.

If you follow the two Golden Rules – **accurate sales forecasts** and **regular meetings** between the people responsible for the four key areas – you are well on the way to getting working capital under control and keeping it there.

Carruthers: But this means change. My people won't like it. And I do not want to upset my wonderful people.
Scroggs: Even when your customers are shouting, your salesmen are cursing, your cheques are bouncing and your bank is foreclosing?
Carruthers: Even then, principles are principles. I suppose you find that disappointing.
Scroggs: On the contrary, I am delighted. I have just started manufacturing forks.

Golden rules

1 Accurate sales forecasts are essential.
2 Involve the relevant people in your company – and have meetings.
3 The control of working capital is the heart of business management.
4 Time is money – speed up the time your money takes to produce results.
5 The debtor/creditor equation is vital.
6 Success can be disastrous – if you are not prepared.
7 The cost of keeping everyone happy can destroy a company – so motivate your staff to keep you in business.

3 Cost, profit and break-even

The profit on a product or a business is determined by just three very simple factors – **cost**, **price** and **volume**. The complication is that each influences the other; cost affects price, price affects volume, and volume affects cost. There is no magic formula for striking the right balance, but there is a technique for giving yourself the best chance, and that technique is **costing**.

It will come as no surprise that our old friend Carruthers is deficient in this technique. Here he is, bankrupt, and being sold off at auction after his company went into receivership. The buyer is Rita Scroggs!

Going ... going ... gone

Auctioneer: Finally, lot 74, Managing Director. Good condition, brain hardly used. Who's going to start us off? . . . Do I hear a hundred pounds . . . ten pounds . . . ten pence?
Scroggs: OK, ten pence. Come along, chum. You're mine.

Carruthers: I do not understand it. I simply do not understand it.
Scroggs: No. I suppose I just felt sorry for you, because I know all about you.
Carruthers: That is not what I do not understand. How can it happen that an intelligent, enterprising man can be declared bankrupt, when he has money in the bank and is selling his goods at a profit?
Scroggs: Quite easily.
Carruthers: What was that?
Scroggs: Tell me about it. After all, we are both in the same business.
Carruthers: But I am up-market and you are down-market.
Scroggs: I know. But then my business is booming and yours is bust.
Carruthers: Isn't it absurd? Is there no justice in business?
Scroggs: No, but there is logic. So tell me about it.
Carruthers: Very well. I had a brilliant idea – one of the greatest creative ideas of the century. Carruthers' Coupled Cutlery. Ideal for buffet lunches, family picnics and camping holidays. The knork – slices the sausage with one end, spears it with the other. The spork – fixes the strawberry on one end, scoops up the cream with the other. The spife – takes the jam

with one end, spreads it with the other. The hiker's friend, the camper's companion. Carruthers' Coupled Cutlery! And what's more, the inventive brilliance was matched by the financial sophistication.
Scroggs: It wasn't.
Carruthers: It was.
Scroggs: I can't wait to hear about it.
Carruthers: Let me demonstrate. I calculated that I could sell my coupled cutlery for £400 a case. And that I could produce and sell ten cases a week – total sales revenue, £4000 a week. But I went into even more detail. I worked out that my costs would be only £2000 a week – for labour, materials and overheads. That meant £2000 a week profit on ten cases. See! Cost – £200 per case, and profit – £200 per case.

Carruthers did his sums and worked out that it would cost him £2000 a week to produce ten cases of Carruthers' Coupled Cutlery. He was also sure he could sell them for £400 a case. This led him to produce a complex and sophisticated diagram.

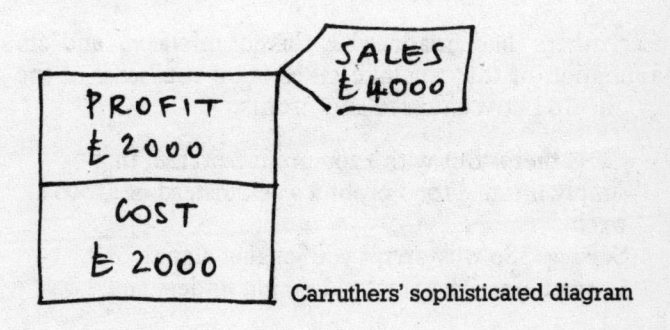

Carruthers' sophisticated diagram

Carruthers was not a man to resist or reject the findings of mathematical science. With this clear proof that he was going to make £2000 a week he went into business. And he did indeed produce cases of coupled cutlery. What is more, he sold them at £400 a case.

>**Scroggs:** So what went wrong?
>**Carruthers:** Nothing. It was just that I only managed to sell five cases a week instead of ten.

But of course a man like Carruthers was not going to be deterred by a little thing like that. He produced a revised diagram.

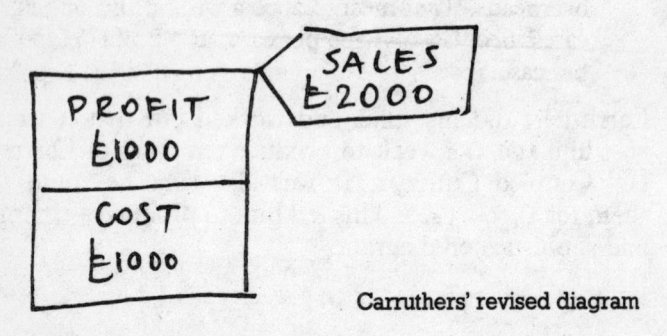

Carruthers' revised diagram

Carruthers had made the classic mistake, and an examination of that mistake takes us to the heart of the relationship between costs and profits.

>**Carruthers:** But with £200 profit per case, that simply meant £1000 profit a week instead of £2000 a week.
>**Scroggs:** So why aren't you jogging along?
>**Carruthers:** That is what I do not understand.

Scroggs: Could you show me how you arrived at that £2000 figure in detail.
Carruthers: You mean *even greater* detail? Very well. Income: ten cases at £400 each – £4000. Expenditure: strip metal, ten consignments, £70 each – £700. Lubricants, packaging and so on – £100. Part-time labour, a bit of extra typing, a bit of help on sales – £200. The three lads at £200 a week each, £600. Overheads and general marketing – £400. Total expenditure – £2000 . . . profit £2000. There. How's that?
Scroggs: Very good. Except that it didn't happen.
Carruthers: Well, it half happened.
Scroggs: Quite so. So would you mind telling me in detail what actually happened?
Carruthers: Why? It's bound to come out at £1000 profit instead of £2000.
Scroggs: Even so.
Carruthers: You've got to spell it out for some people! All right. Income down to £1000 now. Half the metal – er – £350; half the lubricant – £50. Half the part-time labour – £100. Other labour, well, that's three lads at £200 a week each . . .
Scroggs: Why are you still employing three lads, with only half the turnover?
Carruthers: You can't just take on and lay off skilled lads like mine. They'd be off to someone else like a flash. I have to guarantee them their jobs.
Scroggs: You mean they're staff?
Carruthers: Well, I don't eat with them, obviously. But yes – staff. Three at £200 – £600. And overheads still £400.
Scroggs: So the total expenditure is?

Carruthers: £1500.
Scroggs: Very nice. So nice that £2000 take away £1500 makes £1000?
Carruthers: Precisely. What?
Scroggs: £2000 take away £1500?
Carruthers: I don't understand. I'm doing half as much business, but only making a quarter of the profit. There must be a mistake.
Scroggs: There's been a mistake all right. You worked out that ten cases – £4000 worth of sales – cost £2000 to produce and sell and left £2000 profit.

This diagram shows what really happened to Carruthers' profits when he halved his production; they were not halved, they were quartered.

The mistake is obvious. All the same, some obvious mistakes are quite easy to make. The easiest way to make this one is to look back over the previous period when, let us say, you produced 1000 cases at a cost of £200,000, and deduce that your production costs are therefore £200 a case. Wrong – they *were* £200 a case, in the previous period. And they were only £200 *because you produced 1000 cases*. With 800 or 1200 the cost per case would have been different. So to go into a new period assuming that the cost is still £200 per case is a recipe for disaster.

Let's look at Carruthers' costs in detail.

> **Scroggs:** So you spent £400 on overheads and marketing, £600 for the lads – that's £1000. And £1000 for the rest – £200 for part-time labour, £100 for lubricants and so on, and £700 for metal. But if you cut your turnover in half your overheads don't change. They are still £400. And your staff costs don't change – they are still £600. The other costs – metal, lubricants, casual labour, *do* change. They come down from £1000 to £500. But it only leaves you £500 profit.
>
> So that makes your cost per case look just a little bit different. If you're producing only five cases a week instead of ten, costs now take up three-quarters of the price of each case – £300 – and profits are only a quarter – £100.
>
> **Carruthers:** But those are just accountants' figures.
> **Scroggs:** And bank managers' figures. And receivers' figures. And judges' figures.
> **Carruthers:** Well, what is a decent, honest chap supposed to do?
> **Scroggs:** A decent, honest chap can start by

separating his **fixed costs** from his **variable costs**. Remember we compared your forecast turnover of £4000 with your actual turnover of £2000? Let's look at those costs. Some of them didn't change – staff and overheads were the same, whatever the turnover. They're fixed costs.

Anyone who has had to deal with the real costs of a real business will recognise the horrifying oversimplification of Carruthers' costings. Nevertheless some businesses – including some successful businesses – have been started up on the basis of back-of-an-envelope calculations of this sort. But once you get going you are faced with the costs of staying in business as well as the costs of production; and Carruthers had left out of the record some of the latter costs as well as all of the former. So let us take a look at some of the main categories of fixed cost.

1. The inevitable. You cannot get away from paying certain basic fixed costs – wages, rent, rates, insurance, heating, lighting, telephone, stationery, postage and some basic professional fees for legal and financial services. You may also have loan interest (although this may be dealt with separately as a finance charge).
2. Start-up costs. Starting up any new project nearly always involves special extra costs that do not recur once you have got going: making jigs, dies and templates, for example, buying equipment, furnishings and supplying promotional literature. Every business has different start-up costs, but they are always there. They will have to be paid for out of the contribution element in sales before you

show any profits (with job-costing systems, these special items may be treated as a direct expense and charged to the cost of a job).
3 Selling, distribution and administration costs (these are the most frequently underestimated). Once you have customers you have selling costs, even if you have no salesmen. Orders must be taken, recorded, confirmed, dispatched and invoiced; cheques must be reconciled, entered and banked. Sales enquiries must be answered, complaints investigated, delivery errors corrected, late payers reminded, faulty goods replaced or unsatisfactory work done again. All this requires people's time and, unless you have found a way of getting it done for nothing, that means costs.
4 Depreciation. Nearly all equipment wears out. A machine costing £10,000 may be worth nothing in five years' time. If so, that means its value is depreciating at the rate of £2000 a year. You are using it up as surely as you are using the metal it is pressing. That £2000 is money you are spending. Unless you record it as a depreciation cost you are fooling yourself, and you will be in for a big shock in five years' time when the machine packs up and you cannot afford to replace it.
5 Maintenance. Windows break. Roofs leak. Bulbs blow. Paint peels. Pipes leak. Drains get blocked. Machines seize up. Everyone knows these things happen, but you would be surprised how many people fail to allow for them in advance when drawing up costs.

Unforeseen hazards

6 Contingency. A supplier has a strike just as you are waiting for delivery to complete a contract with a time penalty clause. You can get the materials from Germany, but it means a higher price and air freight charges. Or a customer goes bankrupt while owing you a lot of money. Or . . . They will not all happen, but it is extremely foolish to assume that none of them will.

This is a very brief list of the major categories of fixed costs which even the smallest business will incur and must take into account when evaluating any new project. Scroggs develops the theme of fixed and variable costs.

Scroggs: There are, of course, costs which only arose when you produced cutlery – metal and lubricants and so on. These are the **variable** costs: £1000 on ten cases, £500 on five – £100 a case. So your variable costs are £100 a case.

Carruthers: Fascinating. You are telling me that I make £300 profit on each case.

Scroggs: That is not what I am telling you.

Carruthers: What are you telling me?

Scroggs: I am telling you that we are now in a position to look for the missing figure.

Carruthers: What missing figure?

Scroggs: The key figure for any new project. The one figure you have to know before you start.

Carruthers: Which is?

Scroggs: The break-even figure. Look, you worked out that ten cases gave you £2000 profit. Now what was the maximum you could produce a week?

Carruthers: Sixteen. Top whack.

Scroggs: But how many do you have to sell just to stay in business?

Carruthers: Nine? One? Five?

Scroggs: I don't know. Not yet. But we're in a position to work it out. We know each case has a variable cost of £100.

Carruthers: And £300 profit.

Scroggs: Not £300. How can it be profit if you haven't paid the rent or the wages or your heating bills? What about fixed costs?

Carruthers: Ah . . .

Scroggs: That £300 that's left after you've paid the variable costs is a contribution towards the fixed costs. Once you've paid those, it's a contribution to profit. At the moment all we know is that it's £300 contribution. It's the value you and your lads have added to the raw materials that you bought, by turning them into cutlery.

Your fixed costs were £1000, remember. Well, you can think of them as a hole £1000 deep. Each case makes a £300 contribution to filling it. So two cases pay off £600 of the fixed cost. Three pay off £900. And with the four cases, you pay off the last £100 and make £200 profit. If you make a fifth case that week, then that case's £300 contribution is indeed profit – all of it.

So your break-even point in that example is 3.3 cases a week.

Carruthers: You see? I knew it! 3.3 cases a week – I was producing five! I was making a profit. Excuse me, I must go, I'm a success!!!

Scroggs: Wait a minute! I said, 'in that example'. But there was something I left out of that example.

Carruthers: Why?

Scroggs: Because there are some minds that cannot take in more than one idea at a time. If that.

Carruthers: What have we left out?

Scroggs: Depreciation of fixed assets.

Carruthers: Ah, of course.

Scroggs: You understand depreciation? How would you describe it?

Scroggs: Er . . . I'm not awfully good at the describing lark. But I'd be awfully interested to see how you make out.

Scroggs: Thank you. Tell me, how much did you pay for all your machines – cutters, dies, presses and so on?

Carruthers: £40,000. The whole of Aunt Agatha's legacy.

> **Scroggs:** And how long until you have to replace them?
> **Carruthers:** Ages. Ages.
> **Scroggs:** How long?
> **Carruthers:** A good five years.
> **Scroggs:** And then you go out of business?
> **Carruthers:** No. Then I buy some more.
> **Scroggs:** What with?
> **Carruthers:** Profits?
> **Scroggs:** Suppose they're not enough? Suppose you spent them on something else?
> **Carruthers:** All right. Tell me.
> **Scroggs:** Right. 'Depreciation'. You started with Aunt Agatha's legacy – £40,000. And you turned it into machine tools. But it was still worth £40,000 – you just put it into machines instead of the bank. But as you use a machine, you start to use it up, just as if you were spending the money. Each case of cutlery takes a tiny bit of the machine's value with it, as well as the strip metal. It's another cost of production.

And after five years the machine's whole value will have gone. Carruthers will have spent the whole machine. So part of his sales income has to be set against that invisible expenditure of the machine's value. That's depreciation. It may look like money in the bank, but in five years' time he's going to need all of it to replace his machines and stay in business. Using up £40,000 over five years means using up £8000 a year.

And Carruthers will have to allow another £2000 a year for rising prices, because those machines won't still cost £40,000 in five years' time. That means setting aside a total of £200 a week for depreciation.

Scroggs: You've got to be realistic. That hole isn't £1000 deep, it's £1200. Which means that £200 contribution from the fourth case isn't profit after all. It's swallowed up by depreciation. So your break-even point is four cases, not 3.3. Their contribution has to pay for the £400 overheads, £600 labour and £200 depreciation. So there's £1200 of fixed costs and four contributions of £300 each.

Carruthers: So my break-even point is four cases.

Scroggs: So it seems.

Carruthers: Then what is all this bankruptcy charade in aid of? I was turning out five cases. I'm laughing. Aren't I?

Scroggs: Apparently not. Could there by anything you've forgotten?

Carruthers: No.

Scroggs: Tell me how you started this fascinating business.

Carruthers: Ah, what a story! All my own idea. Got a die-maker. Prototype, market tests, re-design. Wonderful publicity campaign, ads, mailshots, the lot. Launched at a buffet lunch served exclusively with Carruthers' Coupled Cutlery. Triumph, triumph.

Scroggs: When was all this?

Carruthers: Just over a year ago.

Scroggs: How much did it all cost?

Carruthers: Well, you don't spoil the ship for a ha'porth of tar . . . £50,000.

Scroggs: And where did that come from?

Carruthers: I got a loan.

Scroggs: Interest rate?

Carruthers: Twenty per cent.

Scroggs: Security?
Carruthers: Machines, patents, trade marks.
Scroggs: Repayable when?
Carruthers: Just over twelve months.
Scroggs: And how much has been repaid?
Carruthers: . . . Nothing.

So what should Carruthers have done? He should have carried out a proper costing, which in this case would have been to use **marginal costing**.

What is marginal costing? To put it technically, it is the cost of producing one more unit at the margin of your output. To put it simply, think of a house with four people living in it. Rent, rates, food, fuel, insurance and general wear-and-tear come to £200 a week – £50 a head. So what is the extra cost if a fifth person comes to stay in the house? Obviously not another £50 – rent, rates and insurance do not go up at all. Fuel and wear-and-tear go up a little, but not much. Food goes up quite a lot. You might find that with a fifth person, the cost of running the house went up from £200 a week to £230 a week. So the marginal cost of having a fifth person to live in the house is £30 a week.

> **Scroggs:** You should have produced a business plan, based on a break-even figure worked out in advance.
> **Carruthers:** You mean like you've just been doing?
> **Scroggs:** Yes. Or there is another way. **Total absorption costing**.
> **Carruthers:** Please, please don't confuse me with information.
> **Scroggs:** It's simple, really. Look, how much would it cost you to produce one case a week?
> **Carruthers:** Ah, I can do that. Fixed costs – £2400,

as I'm paying off my loan. Variable costs – £100. So that's £2500.

Scroggs: And if you produced two cases, what would they cost each?

Carruthers: Simple. Half £2500, which is, er . . .

Scroggs: What about the variable costs on the second case?

Carruthers: As I was saying. Half £2600 which is, er, £1300.

Scroggs: Three cases?

Carruthers: A third of £2600 – I mean, – £2700 er . . .

Scroggs: Four cases? Five cases?

Carruthers: Hang on, hang on, old bean.

Scroggs: It's all right, I've done it for you. Five cases cost £580 each to produce. Six come down to £500. Eight come down to £400 each. And if you get up to sixteen, they're only costing you £250 each.

Carruthers: Ah, £150 contribution per case.

Scroggs: No. £150 profit. The £250 has absorbed all your fixed costs already.

Carruthers: So it has! £150 profit. Good Lord. But where does all this get me?

Scroggs: Well, suppose you can sell ten cases a week. Each case will cost you £340 a case to make a profit. If you charge less, you're in the red. Or you can do it the other way. If you reckon that £400 a case is the most you can charge you can work out how many you've got to produce to break even. If you produce less, you're in the red.

You remember that in the case of the house with four people living in it the marginal cost of a fifth person staying in it was £30 a week, since the overall running cost went up from £200 a week to £230 a week. If you used **total absorption costing**, you would say that the effect of a fifth person staying in it was £30 a week, since the overall running cost went up from £200 a week to £230 a week. So the effect of this fifth person coming to stay was to lower the unit cost from £50 a week to £46 a week. You would reach this figure by taking £200 a week shared between four people (£50 a week each) and changing it to £230 a week shared between five people (£46 each a week).

> **Carruthers:** But if I'd done one of your costings and found out that I had to sell eight cases a week this whole magnificent enterprise would never have started. I knew I couldn't guarantee that.
> **Scroggs:** Yes, a business plan does stop people from starting up doomed projects. But it also gives you a chance to look at the alternatives. Could you have cut your variable costs?
> **Carruthers:** No.
> **Scroggs:** Used less labour?
> **Carruthers:** No.
> **Scroggs:** Charged more per case?
> **Carruthers:** Not a hope.
> **Scroggs:** Charged less per case?
> **Carruthers:** Brilliant! The woman is a commercial genius. Business brain of the century. You're going bankrupt, you must cut your profits.
> **Scroggs:** How many cases would you sell at £300 each?
> **Carruthers:** I'd *sell* a lot.
> **Scroggs:** How many?

Carruthers: Fifteen a week at least.
Scroggs: What would each one cost you if you were making fifteen?
Carruthers: Er . . . £260 . . . wait a minute, that's £40 contribution, I mean profit per case!
Scroggs: Right!
Carruthers: I am a retrospective millionaire.
Scroggs: The bankruptcy courts are full of retrospective millionaires.
Carruthers: But my idea works.
Scroggs: If you're right about selling fifteen cases at £300 each. And if you can actually produce fifteen cases a week. And if you can still keep your fixed costs at £2400. And if you can . . .
Carruthers: Forget the trivialities. I was on to a good thing all along.
Scroggs: You may have been on to a good thing at £300 a case. It seems you were on to a bad thing at £400 a case.
Carruthers: But now I know all about it . . .
Scroggs: Do you know all about it? Tell me.
Carruthers: All right. I will. First, **marginal costing**. You divide your production costs into two different kinds. **Fixed costs**, the ones you have to pay whatever happens, and **variable costs**, the ones you only pay when you produce something. The difference between the variable cost of the product and the price you charge for it is the contribution to fixed costs, until they're all paid off. When they are, that's your break-even figure. After that, they're contribution to profit.

Secondly, there's **total absorption costing**. That way, you take the total costs, fixed and variable, and

divide them by all the different numbers you might sell. That enables you to work out a different 'unit cost' figure for all the different volumes.
Scroggs: Very good indeed. Twelve months too late, but very good all the same. And now if you'll excuse me . . .
Carruthers: Where are you going?
Scroggs: Oh, I've got a little business to sort out. A cutlery business. Lent them £50,000 a year ago. Good security – machines, patents, trade marks – and now they've gone bust.
Carruthers: Really? Why?
Scroggs: Never worked their costs out, never had a business plan. Overpriced their product, and that was that.
Carruthers: Ha! Ha! Never worked their costs out . . .

Golden rules

1 Distinguish between fixed and variable costs.
2 Do not confuse a profit with a contribution to costs.
3 Know your break-even figures for each order.
4 Allow for depreciation in your costings.
5 Produce a business plan – and use it.

4 Budgeting

Carruthers seems to have it made, finally! He is now sitting behind a huge antique desk with a fat cigar and some brandy. A chart on the wall behind him shows sales over several lean years, followed by the current year's sales, which are shooting up, almost off the graph.

Secretary: There's a Miss Rita Scroggs to see you.
Carruthers: Oh yes, send her in.
Scroggs: Hello, Julian. I thought I'd drop in as I was in the area, visiting Granny.
Carruthers: Your Granny? Tell me, how is her egg-sucking technique these days? Give her a few pointers, did you?
Scroggs: There's no need to have a go at me just because I have taught you everything you know. Your problem is that so far I haven't taught you everything *I* know.
Carruthers: There is one thing you don't know. This year, entirely by my own efforts, my enterprise has taken wing. I admit we've had a few lean years, but in the first six months of this year our sales have boomed. In fact, our sales are 50 per cent higher than last year. Way beyond the target forecast. Look at the chart – and we're not even at the end of the year yet. I don't want to boast, but this could be the year of the Rolls-Royce.
Scroggs: It's that bad, is it?
Carruthers: I don't know what you're talking about.

> I now realise that *you* don't know what you're talking about either. Can't you understand? Sales are up!
> **Scroggs:** Yes – up 50 per cent. Were you expecting that?
> **Carruthers:** No, I wasn't. However, I am delighted that it has happened.
> **Scroggs:** This means trouble.
> **Carruthers:** What?
> **Scroggs:** Don't you realise that an unexpected 50 per cent rise in sales can make just as much trouble as an unexpected 50 per cent fall in sales, or a rise in the cost of labour or new materials or rent or tax . . .
> **Carruthers:** So success should be avoided at all costs because it's so disastrous, is that it?
> **Scroggs:** Look, your sales are certainly accelerating, but that doesn't mean to say your profits are going up as well. Can I have at look at your budget?
> **Carruthers:** What an extraordinary question.
> **Scroggs:** You do you have a budget, don't you?
> **Carruthers:** Well, the wife's got one. Nasty little yellow thing, keeps falling off its perch.
> **Scroggs:** No. Bud-get.
> **Carruthers:** Sorry, I thought you said canary. Budget, yes – it's round here somewhere. I remember, I put it in the fridge.

Carruthers takes out his budget from behind the champagne bottles in the fridge. It is last year's budget with 'This year plus 5 per cent' scrawled across it.

It's obvious that Carruthers does not think about his budget very often. But you must have plans to run a successful business – long term strategic marketing ones, short term sales and production ones, and so on. The most important plan of all is your budget. It tells you where you're going and how you're going to get there. It gives you a destination – a target profit – and maps out a route. Other financial documents such as the balance sheet or the profit and loss account look backwards, tell you where you've been and how you got to where you are now. But you can't drive a car by looking out of the back window, and the budget gives you that vital forward view.

Most companies prepare their master budget once every twelve months – a comprehensive plan integrating all the activities, all the costs and revenue, and summarising the target profit for the year ahead. This master budget will be based on a series of mini-budgets, one for each department, according to how the company chooses to carve itself up for budgeting purposes. Whatever the pattern of 'budget centres', all must interlock together to produce the overall picture.

A budget is not a forecast. A forecast is simply an opinion, however well calculated or considered, as to what might happen. The sun might shine tomorrow, Jaguar might sell a million motor cars next year. Both of these are forecasts. A budget, even though it will be based on forecasts and on very sophisticated assumptions and guesses, is a **commitment**. When you make a budget, you commit yourself to a plan or standard of performance upon which lots of other commitments depend. If you budget to sell a million motor cars next year, then you have to commit everything in your organisation to achieving that level of performance. If you can't make that commitment, then you should revise it to something you think you can achieve – and then make a plan you *can* commit yourself to. Otherwise you risk going bust. Which brings us back to Julian Carruthers . . .

>**Scroggs:** This is it, is it? I see you've just slapped 5 per cent on last year's budget. Now, why do you suppose you're so far out on your sales target?
>**Carruthers:** So far *above* our sales target, you mean? Well, I admit I see this as something of a success story. Let me explain. I came up with an absolutely brilliant idea. Cutcrox Co-ordinated Cutlery and Crockery. The square-meal soup set. Now you can't eat soup out of a square soup-plate with a round spoon, and vice versa. So they have to sell as a set, and sell they did.
>
>In fact, to meet the enormous demand, Production are all working overtime – and without a murmur.
>**Scroggs:** I'll bet.
>**Carruthers:** Of course, it's our marketing chaps who are the real heroes. They've been running a massive press and radio advertising campaign, and the response has been, well – frankly, fantastic. In fact, Distribution have had to rent an extra van to cope with the deliveries. So, thanks to our enormous sales our profits are going to be fantastic.
>**Scroggs:** Your sales may well be up 50 per cent, but I very much doubt if your profits will be.
>**Carruthers:** No, our profits will be up 250 per cent!
>**Scroggs:** What?
>**Carruthers:** Let me make it easy for you. Last year our income was £200,000. Of that, £40,000 was profit. This year sales are up 50 per cent, that's £300,000. So profit is going to be £140,000, up by £100,000. You see? Compared with last year's

£40,000 that's up by 250 per cent.
Scroggs: And this is all quite different from your original budget?
Carruthers: Oh yes. This all came as a very pleasant surprise.
Scroggs: Well, you're half right. It is a surprise.
Carruthers: You mean it's not pleasant?
Scroggs: Let's find out. Last year your income was £40,000 above expenditure. But this year, according to your budget at least, expenditure is going to rise by 5 per cent.
Carruthers: But don't forget that, according to my budget, income was going to rise by 5 per cent too. So it's still well ahead of expenditure.
Scroggs: But it didn't happen that way, did it?
Carruthers: No, of course it didn't. Income went up and up and up.
Scroggs: How did it go up so fast?
Carruthers: Sales.
Scroggs: Look – you've been pouring out money to achieve those sales. And in pouring it out you've been increasing your expenditure. How much did your massive advertising campaign cost you?
Carruthers: Oh, that – £80,000. Well, maybe I'm not doing as well as I thought. But I'm still in profit.
Scroggs: Yes, but how much did all that extra overtime cost?
Carruthers: Only about £60,000.
Scroggs: And how about your distribution costs? Renting an extra van, sending stock out by rail?
Carruthers: Yes . . .
Scroggs: How much?
Carruthers: . . . £40,000.

Scroggs: So your costs have shot up by £180,000 and your income has only gone up by £100,000. Now do you see? You're in way over your head. What you're looking at now is not a 50 per cent profit, it's a loss. You're not waving, you're drowning.
Carruthers: How was I supposed to know that that was happening?
Scroggs: By using your budget.

A budget isn't something you just compile and then file. Once you've prepared a budget, however good or bad, you don't put it in the fridge to stop it going off. You use it to manage the business, or your part of it. Any budget is only as good as the work you put in to **create** it in the first place, and then what you do to **monitor** and **control** it. You must consult it regularly and take corrective action where needed to keep on course.

What went wrong for Carruthers – the basic budget mistake – is that he never looked at his budget from one year to the next. It's no good just slapping an across-the-board increase on last year's figures to arrive at this year's figures. And the idea is not to wait until the end of the year to look at this year's budget and see whether you've 'beaten' it. Remember, budgeting is about looking forwards, not backwards. About planning for the wine you will buy to celebrate the end of the year, not waiting until 31 December to see whether you want to drown your sorrows or paint the office red.

Carruthers is totally surprised by a 'boom' in his sales over the last year and interprets this as good fortune without stopping to explore the consequent effects throughout his business. A 50 per cent increase in sales revenue doesn't mean an automatic increase in profit, and he spends an extra £80,000 on advertising, £60,000 on overtime and £40,000 on extra distribution, without any check on whether he can really afford to. He thinks he's going to be swimming in champagne but he might in fact be drowning in a rather stormy sea.

> **Scroggs:** Your budget is the most precise tool you've got for measuring your company's performance. So use it. Look, your departments have been spending every penny that came from sales and now they're spending money that isn't even there.
> **Carruthers:** Good point. But how will my budget help?
> **Scroggs:** A budget shows where you're going. Of course your sales chart is important, but that only shows you where you've been. You can't set out on a journey and only look backwards. Better still, plot a course, and that's what your budget should be.

Carruthers: So my budget is my course through the future, is it?
Scroggs: Yes, although yours is not a very good one, is it? I mean, if you were planning a five-mile journey, and you ended up fifty miles away, I'd say you'd plotted a pretty rotten course, wouldn't you?
Carruthers: Well, room for improvement certainly.

When you prepare a budget, you work out all the sources of revenue and all the areas of costs; decide what you think you can sell, for how much, and what it will cost you to do so. But what other people think is as important as what you think and it can't be over-emphasised that good budgeting is as much about the proper handling of **people** as it is about the proper handling of **money**. Anyone who is preparing a budget must consult his colleagues, his subordinates and his superiors. These people must be involved, to help decide what yardsticks should be used and whether a proposed budget is realistically feasible. It is important that other people should participate in the standard-setting process for two main reasons. First, it helps you set more realistic standards. Second, it makes it much harder for people to complain at a later stage if the plan doesn't work out and they have to alter things. Involvement from the start will increase motivation and help boost morale if the going gets rough. In a similar vein, budgeting is a vital part of delegation. If you give people discretion to make their own decisions to achieve agreed goals, then performance against budget is a good method of assessment.

Scroggs: Tell me, Julian, how did you construct your budget?
Carruthers: Easy. I cast an eye over last year's

figures and saw they were about 5 per cent up across the board on the previous year, so I carefully slapped on another 5 per cent and Bob's your uncle – this year's budget.

Scroggs: But you were 50 per cent out on sales, and 250 per cent out on profit and loss, so you say.

Carruthers: Yes, but what you're not taking into account is . . . tell me about budgets.

Scroggs: Right. What do you need to make a budget?

Carruthers: Luck?

Scroggs: Judgement.

Carruthers: I see. Of course. I use my judgement.

Scroggs: Wrong. You use everybody's judgement. Take advantage of your staff's knowledge, experience and judgement to assess the factors that are likely to influence the company's performance. Why don't we go back to the beginning of the year and make your budget all over again?

Carruthers: Very well, if you think it will help.

Scroggs: Right. These are the things you've got to do with a budget. You construct it. You make the best guess of the year's income and expenditure. Then you co-ordinate it. Check that each department's plans mesh in with each other's and don't conflict with them. And then you use it to control business, month by month all through the year. Now let's take these one at a time. First?

Carruthers: Construct.

Scroggs: Right. Now you construct your budget by considering income, expenditure and profit. So what are you going to aim for?

Carruthers: Easy. Income – one billion pounds,

expenditure – nil, profit – one billion.
Scroggs: No. That's unrealistic.
Carruthers: It's very attractive.
Scroggs: But you have to consider reality.
Carruthers: All right. Er . . . how about 6 per cent on last year's budget . . . 7 per cent? All right – 27 per cent. No, no – 492.31 per cent.
Scroggs: Look, you can't create your budget on your own. You need the knowledge and judgement of the people who are going to be creating the income and expenditure and profit. So, to construct your budget you first of all consult your departments – to keep it simple let's say Production, Marketing and Distribution. You need their estimates of performance, their mini-budgets to help you create your master budget.

The sales forecast gives the revenue target. What did Carruthers do when he was preparing his new sales forecast? Easy. 'I cast an eye over last year's figures, saw they were about 5 per cent up across the board, so I carefully slapped on another 5 per cent and Bob's your uncle – this year's budget.'

Using as much market intelligence as possible, Carruthers should have looked at the size of the market last year, considered anything likely to alter the size of it this year, found out what the competition were up to, sought out any changes in social habits or dining behaviour likely to affect his product sales and so on. Above all, he should have talked to his sales force. What do they think they can sell?

There will be guesswork and assumptions, but since you will be stuck with the figures you decide upon, you should aim to be as realistic as possible. If Carruthers had more than one product, say knives, forks and spoons, his sales forecast would necessarily become more complex – taking into account not only the quantities of each product to be sold, but also the mix between different products and their relative prices.

Budget preparing is a dialogue

Scroggs: So, you'd better start with your expected sales. Why not consult your marketing department?

Carruthers: Hello? Carruthers here. Tell me, how many cases can you sell a day?
Marketing manager: Well, if we carry on with present sales schedules I reckon we could shift fifty, sixty, seventy . . . oh no, let's call it sixty. We can definitely shift sixty cases a day.
Carruthers: Sixty cases a day at £20 per case! We're looking at £1200 per day income here. Hooray! Now . . .

Carruthers: Production? Do you think you could come up with sixty a day for us?
Production manager: Eighty.
Carruthers: Pardon?
Production manager: Well, me and the lads could knock out eighty cases a day – no danger.
Carruthers: Eighty? My word, at £20 per case that's £1600 income . . .

Carruthers: Could your distribution chaps handle eighty cases **a day**?
Distribution manager: Eighty? A hundred more like.
Carruthers: One hundred? That's £2000 a day. This is wonderful.

Carruthers is now heading for worse trouble than ever. It is pointless for each division within a company to calculate its own budget and then have them all lumped together. Budgets have to fit together, which demands co-ordination.

You have to start with your **major limiting factor**,

which for many companies is likely to be 'how many can we make?'. Or there could be other constraints which impose a natural limit on the business. Having decided what the limiting factor is, you can gear everything else to suit.

The **cash budget** will always be an important variable too. This plans the availability and flow of money, lets you know what you can afford and when. In most larger companies, this will be the province of the management accountants, but it will play an important role in the co-ordination process. Cash, too, could therefore be a limiting factor.

Let's take a closer look at how, under tuition, Julian Carruthers managed to co-ordinate his budget.

> **Carruthers:** Miss Scroggs! We can distribute a hundred cases a day – that's £2000.
> **Scroggs:** You can only make eighty.
> **Carruthers:** True . . . but that's still £1600 a day.
> **Scroggs:** And that is what we call a limiting factor. In this case the limiting factor is how many cases can you sell? Answer, sixty cases a day.
> **Carruthers:** Still, £1200 a day. That's not bad, is it?
> **Scroggs:** You tell me. How much will it cost you?
> **Carruthers:** Let's have a think. For a start there's overheads – about £100 a day, and next there's production – at a rough guess . . .
> **Scroggs:** Don't make a rough guess. Find out.

> **Carruthers:** It's me again. How much would you say it would cost to produce these sixty cases a day?
> **Production manager:** Like I said, we could do more. But for sixty it would cost us £500 a day.
> **Carruthers:** Not bad. Now . . .

Carruthers: What would it cost you to cope with sixty cases a day?
Marketing manager; For sixty cases a day – a mere £500.
Carruthers: Only £500? Good, good. Now for Distribution . . .

Distribution manager: £300 a day – that's all it would cost.
Carruthers: Excellent, excellent. Well, look at this, Miss Scroggs – £500 a day and £500 a day and £300 a day plus £100 for the overheads, that's all it costs.
Scroggs: And added together?
Carruthers: Added together – £1400 a day.
Scroggs: To produce sixty cases at £20 each, making . . .
Carruthers: Now wait a minute. There's something very wrong here.
Scroggs: No, so far you've done everything right, you've constructed your budget.
Carruthers: But it says I'm going to make a loss.
Scroggs: So what do you do?
Carruthers: Co-ordinate?
Scroggs: Go on, then. Co-ordinate.
Carruthers: I'd absolutely love to, but I don't know what it means.
Scroggs: It means that you adjust each department's expenditure budget in the light of the others', and of the overall income budget, until they all fit together into a workable plan that leaves you a decent profit. Why not call a meeting?
Carruthers: Good idea.

Later . . .

Marketing manager: Excuse me, Mr Carruthers, but I was just thinking – shoot me down in flames if I'm wrong here – but I reckon we could shift 120 cases a day if we went into an intensive radio and press advertising campaign.
Carruthers: 120, eh? £2400 a day!
Production manager: 200.
Carruthers: Pardon?
Production manager: If you can get us an extra machine press and if the lads work overtime, you're looking at 200 cases a day.
Carruthers: £4000!
Distribution manager: We can't handle that.
Carruthers: You can't?
Distribution manager: I told you – 100 cases a day, top whack. But of course, if we had another van, we could deliver 250 a day.
Carruthers: £5000!
Scroggs: It'll cost you.
Carruthers: Yes, but I can work that out. Limiting factor – sales of 120 cases a day, that's £2400 a day. Now, that's against overheads at £100 a day, then there's production at £500 a day, plus leasing a new machine press at £300 a day, plus overtime at £100 a day. Next – marketing at £500 a day plus press advertising at £100 a day, plus radio advertising at £400 a day. Finally – distribution at £300 a day, plus extra transport at £300 a day. So we've got income £2400, expenditure . . .
Scroggs: £2600.
Carruthers: Oh crumbs – that's still a loss.

Distribution manager: Excuse me, but remember I told you we could deliver 100 cases a day if we were without the extra van.
Carruthers: 100 cases? Well, how about Marketing? What would it cost you to sell 100 cases?
Marketing manager: Well, we could still move 100 cases if we forgot the radio advertising and just went for the press advertising.
Carruthers: And Production?
Production manager: We could produce 100 without a new machine, but the lads would still have to work overtime.
Carruthers: So, to produce 100 cases a day at £20 each – namely £2000 income – it would cost £100 a day overheads, £500 a day production plus only £100 for overtime as we won't be needing the extra machine. Add on £500 a day marketing, plus only £100 for press advertising as we're not going for radio. And finally – distribution – £300 plus nothing because distribution say they can deliver 100 cases a day in the first place, so that's an income of £2000 against an expenditure of £1600 – that's £400 profit!
Scroggs: Mr Carruthers, I'm very impressed. Are you happy?
Carruthers: I'm modestly exuberant, I can tell you that.
Scroggs: What about everyone else?
Carruthers: Well, I can tell them that too.
Scroggs: No, no. Are they satisfied with your plans? Don't forget they have to commit themselves to your budget if it's going to work.
Carruthers: Commit themselves? Oh yes . . .
Scroggs: You won't get the best out of them if

they're not satisfied that the budget's sensible. Constructing a budget isn't just about handling **figures**, it's about handling **people** too. So when you've constructed the budget, made your best guess and then co-ordinated it so everyone agrees about the future pattern of performance, you can move on to the last stage. Where are you going?
Carruthers: I'm going to put the budget in the fridge. I don't want it to go off.
Scroggs: But it's a tool, remember? You've still got to use it – that's the last stage.
Carruthers: How? No, don't tell me . . .
Scroggs: Control.

There's no guarantee that everything will work out according to plan. But once agreed to, **the master budget must be adhered to** – not as a straitjacket, but as a decision-making tool. If you've done the job properly and created an accurate budget, your goal must be to stick to it, however hard to bear it may sometimes seem.

If you don't do this you risk damaging the company. 'Beating' the sales budget, for example, can give nasty shocks to Production and Distribution if they can't keep up, or can't keep up at an economical cost. Could the sales budget have been more accurate to start with? Or, if you generate surplus cash, you may take the finance director by surprise and land the company with higher tax bills. Of course, it's better to beat the budget than to be beaten by it, but the best thing is to be spot on.

So **performance must be monitored**. 'How are we doing?' 'Are we getting to where we said we would?' These are key questions to be asked if the budget, and the business, is to be controlled.

Carruthers: So how do I control my budget?
Scroggs: Well, are you just going to turn out 100 cases every day for the whole year?
Carruthers: No. We'll sell more at Christmas and June.
Scroggs: June?
Carruthers: Wedding presents for the June brides, bless 'em. And February and August are slack months.
Scroggs: And costs?
Carruthers: Definitely.
Scroggs: How will that affect costs?
Carruthers: Oh, you mean bigger sales in June mean bigger marketing and distribution costs in April and bigger production costs in March. That sort of thing?
Scroggs: Exactly. So why not go back to the beginning of this year and work out costs, department by department and month by month.
Carruthers: And sales
Scroggs: And sales. Right. It's January again.
Carruthers: Happy old year!
Scroggs: We'll see about that. Now, you've **constructed** your budget, **co-ordinated** your budget and you've got **commitment** to your budget. Now you have to **control** the budget month by month.
Carruthers: Right. January sales budget – £40,000.
Scroggs: Actual?
Carruthers: Spot on.
Scroggs: Costs?
Carruthers: Overheads – £2000, production – £12,000, marketing – £12,000, distribution – £6000. That's £32,000.
Scroggs: Actual?

Carruthers: Spot on again.
Scroggs: Very good. Variance?
Carruthers: No thanks, never touch them . . . what's a variance?
Scroggs: The difference between budgeted performance and actual performance.

The frequency with which a manager should monitor his or her budget and check for **variances** will vary, often according to his or her level within the organisation. To compare just three different levels, for example: the production supervisor or salesperson on the road might check his or her performance daily, the production or sales manager might check weekly and the director on the board might monitor monthly.

The key determinant is: how quickly do you need to know about variances in order to be able to do something about them?

Having discovered a variance you must ask what caused it. Have we lost orders? Have we spent too much on raw materials, or used more materials than we thought we would to achieve a given level of output – a variance on the 'yield'? Have we spent too little or too much on promotion? The nature of the variances will clearly differ according to the nature of the company and the budget. The vital point is to know about them, with sufficient time and information to do something about them.

Watch out too for variances which arise through bad timing rather than bad budgeting. In other words, you may overspend in March because you had to incur costs which you had expected to come through in April. But this will sort itself out by the beginning of May. This type of 'phasing' variance can occur particularly in sales.

If you have a booming month, be careful to check that it's not caused by orders which you would have had anyway, simply brought forward. Otherwise you might have a nasty hole later in the year, which you hadn't allowed for.

> **Scroggs:** So. Nil variance for January. February?
> **Carruthers:** Er . . . sales budget – £36,000. Actual – £40,000. Success! I told you.
> **Scroggs:** Costs?
> **Carruthers:** Well, budget at £32,000, actual costs – £34,000.
> **Scroggs:** Why?
> **Carruthers:** Production was up a bit.
> **Scroggs:** Variance?
> **Carruthers:** Well – sales up £4000, costs up £2000. Variance – £2000.
> **Scroggs:** Positive variance – £2000. Now, March. Costs?
> **Carruthers:** Budget – £36,000. Actual – £42,000. I told Production that they could lease that extra machine after all.
> **Scroggs:** Sales?
> **Carruthers:** Down £4000. Costs up £6000. Er. Variance – £10,000.
> **Scroggs:** Negative variance. Running variance?
> **Carruthers:** What?
> **Scroggs:** Well, it's obvious, isn't it? You have no variance in January, and gained £2000 in February. So your running, or cumulative, variance was positive to the tune of £2000. In March you dropped £10,000 against budget, so at the end of March your running variance is £10,000 negative, plus of course

the February surplus – so that makes £8000 negative. Now, April.

Carruthers: Sales up £2000. Costs up £10,000. (Distribution – extra transport.) Negative variance – £8000. Running variance – £16,000.

Scroggs: May?

Carruthers: Sales £4000 down. Oh no . . . costs £16,000 up – the TV campaign. Negative variance – £20,000. Running variance – £36,000.

Scroggs: Negative.

Carruthers: All right, all right.

Scroggs: June?

Carruthers: Ah, the June brides. Sales down £14,000? They must have been slimming. Costs up £2000 – there was a rent review.

Scroggs: Negative variance – £16,000. Running negative variance – £52,000. £4000 loss instead of a £48,000 profit. There goes the Rolls-Royce.

Carruthers: I see what you mean. What can I do?

Scroggs: Control. Losing control means you must **review**, **react** and **revise**. First **review**.

Carruthers: We've done that.

Scroggs: Well, **react**.

Carruthers bursts into tears.

Scroggs: That's reasonable. But we must also do something.

Carruthers: Do you mean reduce costs? Cut back on advertising, sell the new van, postpone re-equipment?

Scroggs: Or increase sales. Boost advertising in the most promising region. Or try a price cut, or an export drive. You see, there are positive ways of getting the business back on course as well as negative ways. But what matters is to react in time.

But in reacting to variance in the budget, managers can't just sigh or smile. They have to react or report to everyone else who needs to know. Since every element in a budget has consequences for every other – if it's been properly co-ordinated – it's very important to keep people in the know. For example, a production variance could occur if a machine failed. If this were likely to cause prolonged problems, Production should let Marketing know. Otherwise Marketing might commit the company to orders which can't be met, or spend money unwittingly advertising products it can't deliver.

Don't just react to the news of someone else's variance with 'Oh, what rotten luck'. What does this mean for your bit of the business? What corrective action needs taking? If you lose a big order you were expecting, don't just sit and moan. You either need to find a replacement order, or revise all the budgets accordingly.

> **Scroggs:** Finally, at the last stage, **revise** your budget.
> **Carruthers:** You mean change the budgeted expenditure from July up to December?
> **Scroggs:** And the budgeted income. In other words, change all the figures you now realise are going to be wrong.

Don't compile then file. **Monitor continuously**. Then take control action as appropriate either to get the budget back on to its original budget commitments or to take account of the new facts.

Although the management accountant can draw attention to variances when they occur, it's down to the managers responsible to take the necessary action – and above all, to decide which action to take.

Much will depend on how significant the variance is. Remember that variances can go either way, too much or too little, positive or negative. A favourable variance can cause just as many problems as an unfavourable one, if it's a significant amount. In every case, action will be needed. Should we increase advertising expenditure to boost sales? Should we increase production to meet sales figures higher than budgeted? Should Marketing be cut back because Production can't keep up? Should the whole budget be revised to meet the new position?

> **Carruthers:** You mean I should do another budget?
> **Scroggs:** He's got it! By George, he's got it!
> **Carruthers:** Still, that will take some working out. Hold on . . .
> **Scroggs:** Yes
> **Carruthers:** I could have another get-together with the lads. Consult, create and co-ordinate and then use the new budget to control again.
> **Scroggs:** At last!
> **Carruthers:** Now I understand budgets. The budget is the company's course through the future created by the company. **Construct, co-ordinate, control**, and to control your budget you've got to **review, react** and **revise**. I also now understand that my buoyant sales chart may not be quite the good news I thought it was. However, there is still hope.
> **Scroggs:** Indeed there is. Until the next time?
> **Carruthers:** Thank you, Miss Scroggs. By the way, how are things with you? Ticking over all right?

Scroggs: Mustn't grumble. Branched out, actually. Entirely new line.
Carruthers: Really, what are you selling now, then?
Scroggs: Business training manuals. Cheerio.

Golden rules

1 A budget is a tool – not an ornament.
2 A budget is only as good as the work put in to create it in the first place.
3 Prepare your budgets in consultation with others. Construct, co-ordinate, control.
4 A budget is not a forecast, it is a commitment.
5 Compare your 'actuals' against your budget regularly, and examine the variances.
6 Never be afraid to re-budget as circumstances change. Review, react, revise.

Video Arts
World Leaders in Video Training Programmes

For information about hiring or buying
Video Arts training films please contact:

Video Arts Ltd
Dumbarton House
68 Oxford Street
London W1N 9LA

Tel: 071 637 7288
Fax: 071 580 8103

Other Video Arts books available from Mandarin:

Working With People

Do you know how to get your point of view across effectively, without giving offence or creating opposition, and knowing you are being listened to properly? This is the art of assertiveness. Do you know how to get the best out of your colleagues at meetings, ensuring that valuable contributions from others are encouraged in the best way? And in those vital one-to-one exchanges can you appraise others accurately so that both parties benefit; or cope with discipline problems; or deliver bad news constructively? This book is about the human side of management, recognising that working relationships are the key to success.

Are You a Leader?

There was a General whose men said they would follow him anywhere, but only out of curiosity. Do you know where you are going and do your colleagues know too? Taking decisions at the right time; having the courage *not* to take a decision; getting commitment from others; running a meeting for the benefit of all its members; focusing not just on your business but the wider context in which it operates – these are all qualities of leadership in business. This book shows how you as a manager can learn leadership skills, changing your role from a static to a dynamic one while enlisting the co-operation of your colleagues at the same time.

Video Arts Books Available from Mandarin

While every effort is made to keep prices low, it is sometimes necessary to increase prices at short notice. Mandarin Paperbacks reserves the right to show new retail prices on covers which may differ from those previously advertised in the text or elsewhere.

The prices shown below were correct at the time of going to press.

☐	7493 1832 5	**Are you organised?**	£4.99
☐	7493 1827 9	**Are you a leader?**	£4.99
☐	7493 1837 6	**Working with people**	£4.99
☐	7493 1950 X	**Doing business on the phone**	£4.99
☐	7493 1949 6	**Success at selling**	£4.99
☐	7493 1951 8	**Managing money**	£4.99
☐	7493 0095 7	**So you think you can cope with customers?**	£5.99
☐	7493 1043 X	**So you think you can sell?**	£5.99

All these books are available at your bookshop or newsagent, or can be ordered direct from the address below. Just tick the titles you want and fill in the form below.

Cash Sales Department, PO Box 5, Rushden, Northants NN10 6YX.
Fax: 01933 414047 : Phone: 01933 414000.

Please send cheque, payable to 'Reed Book Services Ltd.', or postal order for purchase price quoted and allow the following for postage and packing:

£1.00 for the first book, 50p for the second; **FREE POSTAGE AND PACKING FOR THREE BOOKS OR MORE PER ORDER.**

NAME (Block letters) ....

ADDRESS ....

....

☐ I enclose my remittance for ....

☐ I wish to pay by Access/Visa Card Number

Expiry Date

Signature ....

Please quote our reference: MAND